Surviving a Blue Zoo

Surviving a Blue Zoo

A Little Silly, a Little Angry,
and Sometimes Sane Poems
and Situations

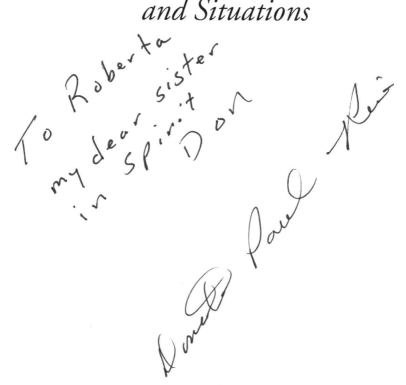

To Roberta
my dear sister
in spirit Don

Donald Paul Rice

Donald Rice

Original artwork by Ruth Young and Donald Rice.

Print information available on the last page.

Rev. date: 05/14/2018

To order additional copies of this book, contact:
Xlibris
1-888-795-4274
www.Xlibris.com
Orders@Xlibris.com
779225

Prologue

It's a little silly that I should have expected my life to be Storybook like, when nothing I've encountered in it has been of the storybook genre. In my heart and mind I've desired the storybook life all along the way, but found nothing in my world to support or guide my desires for it. A storybook life as was read to me in early childhood, and as heard on radio programs and seen on television programs when I was a child, failed to blossom. What was read to me and what I read, when I learned to read, was as elusive as trying to catch fish with my hands. I did actually try to catch fish by hand in Shaker Lake, located in Shaker Heights Ohio on a hot summer day in 1958, but eventually we kids participating in the activity were chased away by Shaker police probably not wanting to explain kids found drowned in the lake. We'd return to east one hundred fortieth street to Robert Fulton elementary school playground and talked about the big fish we tried catch. Just as elusive were the lifestyles of those individuals on radio and television programs. Toss in poor choices due to disillusionment and "Bingo!", a little silly, a little angry, and sometimes sane blossoms.

I used to be a little angry when I compared The United States Constitution, Bill of Rights, and recommendations of the Ten Commandments (if we choose to follow the ways of Christianity) to what I observed and lived daily. The direct and not so direct discrimination, hate, lack of compassion, and empty promises to a culture that had had as much to do with the growth of the country as any other group was obvious. Reality left me a little silly, a little angry, and sometimes sane.

Maturation of my sanity allows me to recognize the fact that so many have no idea why they hate the New World Generated people. Many people of this country don't realize the Confederate civil war ideology is still trying to justified "us" being less than them. Hence, institutionalized and family generated slander of those that didn't want to live as slaves by those that wanted to own people. The Civil War was and is about slavery, results of, or whitewashing of, no matter what spin is put on it today. Truth left me a little silly, a little angry, and sometimes sane.

Set For Life

A Short Story

Paul entered the fenced in parking lot of the shop where he was employed as a mechanic, repairing trailers in various stages of damage that had been used by semi trucks to transport goods across the country. He looked across the vast parking lot at the trailers that had been repaired and were waiting to be picked up, and the ones to be repaired. He assessed the damage of each one he felt would be assigned to him. His last assignment had been replacing fifth wheels on twenty six trailers. Before that it had been lining the interior of about fifty trailers with steel sidings and bulkheads. It seemed that he had established his place in the shop as an interior and undercarriage repair mechanic.

Paul had begun his career as a the shop clean up guy, sweeping out bays after mechanics had completed jobs, fetching tools for the established mechanics, assisting with jobs as his name was called out throughout the shop to do so. The foreman, Jack, seemed to take a liking to Paul. He showed his caring for Paul by giving him small jobs to repair, talking him through each procedure, and having him come in early and teaching him to weld, using scrap metal. Paul was a very fast learner, and eager to do his very best at every reasonable request made of him.

Paul's eagerness to do well could be traced back his mother's teachings and to Paul's military days with the Eighty Second Airborne

Division at Fort Bragg North Carolina. He always identified himself when meeting other paratroopers, by reciting his place within the unit by saying, "Eighty Second - Three Two Five". The Three Two Five was Paul's unit within the "Famous Eighty Second Airborne Division" as it read on the sign entering Fort Bragg. Paul was an Infantryman, which was of very little use in the civilian world, except for the work ethic. Paul worked as if every request made of him was a personal assignment, and nothing mattered until he had completed that assignment.

After leaving the military Paul worked one labor job to the next, never really having a feeling of contributing to his life or society, just simply life at the bottom. The bottom of the pay scale was what he began to expect from any job, which he usually found at the Ohio Bureau of employment. If he got tired of a job, he would visit the Bureau and try another field of work. He was employed in many areas, from laundry labor to cleaning carbon from the inside of oil refinery tanks that stood at the tops of towers that were visible from a bridge overlooking the area in Cleveland, Ohio. Paul really like that job because he worked alone and it was high enough in the air where very few would choose to visit him while he worked.

This job was short lived however, when some workers found out he wasn't a union member and had to be let go at the end of the day. Then it was back to one labor job after another for some months. Paul had nothing against labor work, he just felt that it wasn't what he wanted to do in life.

One day while visiting his mother's home, she told him of a place named Gitee Equipment on East ninety third street in Cleveland, it had been the old Cleveland Transit System car barn (buses). Paul went there the next day, and was hired on the spot by Joe the foreman. Paul watched his life develop into a path of growth, he didn't know where it would take him, but it was growth. Paul made friends while working at the company and looked forward to going to work each day, and hanging out with his co workers at the bar next door to the shop after work. Things were very comfortable for Paul until the Friday when paychecks were passed out, and all employees were told that it was their last day of work "The shop is closing", they were told by Joe. Paul was stunned and only saw himself going back to labor job after labor job.

Paul thought to himself "This can't go on". During his days in the military he had always wanted to be a medic, but his military life was in a "Weapons Squad" in an Infantry Company, and Battle Group in the nineteen sixties at Fort Bragg. It seemed to him that now would be a good time to apply to Nursing School. Paul obtained a Verification for Education from The Veterans Administration in Downtown Cleveland. Paul applied at the Cuyahoga Community College Metro Campus in Cleveland. He took the ACT and was accepted into the Nursing Program. The two most demanding efforts he had ever had challenge him in life up to that point, mentally and physically, becoming a member of the Eighty Second Airborne Division, and becoming a Registered Nurse. So proud was Paul as he walked across the stage and received his Associate Degree in Science. Paul was certain he heard his mother's cheer, out of the mass of friends and relatives of graduates who were attending graduation. Paul now had new purpose and room to grow in any direction his talents could take him.

Paul married a fellow Nursing student, bought his mother a home, and then bought a small farm where he would start and raise a family, though he and his wife continued to work as nurses. This was a long way from the Lee seville housing projects, where he had lived for much of his childhood. Paul never forgot those days and always wanted to do for those needing a helping hand, but Paul wanted to do it it in a big way. He often thought of having a facility called "Study Hall", a place for kids to study and have access to research material; an environment or support to properly address learning and research situations for children that lacked it in the home.

Another thought that teased Paul's mind was to develop a community called "The Garden". It would be a community of multicultural, multiethnic, and multiracial families. A community absent of prejudice and stereotyping, but having a feeling of oneness, all are in one, one is in all. One was more realistic than the other. Study Hall was a much more realistic endeavor. In addition to his career as a nurse, a husband, a father, and a gentleman farmer, these were his desired way to give back to society, for what society had given him. Between financial, work and family demands on his time, it would have taken a miracle to achieve either goal in his lifetime.

Paul's life became one of routine, certainly not boring but one exciting, yet predictable. In his chosen profession, there were many women who found the handsome married man quite desirable. Women of all persuasions, and yes both married and single found him to be quite the individual with whom to have a fling, short or long term, and very rarely did Paul have to pursue a woman. Most seemed to engage him as a break from the mundane, and they usually became close friends even after a cessation of a fling, though another fling may be incurred at anytime. Paul's marriage became a marriage of two dedicated parents committed to the acts and appearance of what their married life should be, yet they both had outside interest; interest known to each other but never openly acknowledged by either.

Their children suspected but never made inquiries concerning their parents outside activities. They lived the life of most children in their environment, and were provided with the love of both parents. As the children got older, Paul began to enter contest, in hopes of winning big and being set for life, so that he may someday realize one of his dreams. One contest especially caught his attention, one of winning thousands of dollars each week for life. Paul thought gleefully, "If I could win that I know I could at least realize my "Study Hall" dream. He entered the contest year after year, until he began entering it out of habit. One day he was sitting at home watching youtube, because he found more truth there than on News Shows. For some time he had realized that Television had no obligation for truthfulness, only to entertain and gather sponsors support, and the sponsors chose what was News and how it was to be presented. This particular day his doorbell rang, and it had happened, Paul had won Thousands of dollars each week for the rest of his life. He could finally be set for life.

The experience was an exercise in euphoria, with a storm of papers needing to be signed, and releases of all types. It didn't matter much to Paul what he had to sign. All he knew was that he arrived there in that office with nothing and was leaving there, set for life. One form did cause Paul to take a quick, questionable look, but he arrived there with nothing, and was leaving there, set for life. The form seemed to have something to do with an insurance beneficiary. He just blew it off and continued to make plans for his "Study Hall" in his thoughts. Thoughts of a possible legacy in the city he loved so much, Cleveland, Ohio.

Paul began to think on a much larger scale. He thought to himself, why not get others that had been winners in Thousands Each Week for Life involved in his plan for making a safe place for children with environmental challenges to learning, in effect, his idea of an independent, after school center, encouraging learning opportunities. All he had to do is find others like himself, and get them to invest in his plan for a safe after school learning center in Cleveland.

Locating the people turned out to be a challenge, so he enlisted the talents of a tech savvy individual who wanted to be included in the venture. With the help of that person he was able to get phone numbers and addresses of those in or near Ohio that had won "Thousands Each Week for Life". Sadly, those that he had initially contacted were either dead or dying, some by accident and others by less than common diseases. He met a relative of one of the deceased, and learned that the corporation running the contest had paid for the funeral of their loved one. The relative had learned that the corporation had an insurance policy on the deceased for several hundred thousands dollars. They told Paul that it was so sad that the person had only collected his Thousands of Dollars a Week, for only three months before he was killed by a pack of stray canines while jogging in Woodhill Park. That was just the first of many that had died by an accident or by an illness that was usually fatal. Many had died within six months of winning.

Paul's findings began to cause him concern and the concern turned to fear when he noticed that a woman who had befriended him began to suggest using drugs, this was out of the question for him. Then she began to suggest fishing and hunting trips. Paul began to equate her suggestions with the insurance policy he'd signed during the required form signings which he had participated.

After winning his Thousands Each Week for Life, his suspicions grew into a full blown paranoid state. He broke off all contact with the woman. He began to avoid contact with others, warning his family about anyone that may have questions about his habits or whereabouts. Paul was sure that by this time he was being followed, but he thought to himself that he was being too paranoid. After thinking that he may be too paranoid, he remembered a saying he once heard ("Just because I'm paranoid doesn't mean that someone is not out to get me.") Paul's survival instincts kicked in, he remembered the woods near where he grew up, in Lee Seville and Miles area in Cleveland, and also the woods in Northeast Ohio near Andover.

His love for the outdoors as a child, and his exposure to the wilderness with his uncle, and his military teachings made those two areas very comfortable places for Paul to exist in until he could expose what he believed was a scheme to profit from the deaths of those winners in the Thousands Each Week for Life contests. The individuals would be promised several thousands of dollars a week for the rest of their lives, and during the period of signing "required" forms, all would sign an additional form naming the corporation and its organizers as beneficiaries to life insurance policies signed by each winner, several hundred thousands of dollars. So in the end each winner may collect up to forty or fifty thousand dollars total, followed by an unexpected demise.

Paul quickly gathered what survival equipment he could obtain on short notice and headed for the wooded areas of Northeast Ohio, after arranging for direct deposit for his winnings to an account to which he and his wife had access.

He was sure he was being followed, so he abandoned his vehicle near Harts, Ohio and took off on foot. He noticed two cars passing up and down route six, the road leading out of Harts as he made his way within wooded areas and paralleled the road. He finally made it to a State Park area. He was surprised to see the two cars already patrolling in the area.

Paul was tired, and after fishing for a meal, chose to camp in the wooded area north of Drover between Lake road and route ten. There he made camp, and curled up under a tree root overhang that made sort of a small cave like area. Paul dozed, but was awakened in the middle of the night by footsteps, a pair of footsteps. He scooted to the edge of his overhang cave and saw a man and a woman in military type gear. It seems that his movement caught their attention. They moved towards him, and he wormed his way to the back of the

Tree root cave, the name he had given the spot where he slept. As they approached he lunged at the man and drove a spiked stick he had whittle into the man's throat. The woman drove a knife into Paul's back all the way to the hilt, he turned and drove a second spiked stick into her abdomen. She stumbled away, as did Paul, each in different directions. Paul curled up in a thick clump of vegetation. He could hear the woman moaning and stumbling in the night. Paul felt a peace come over him, he wasn't sure whether it was sleep or death, whatever it was, it engulfed him.

Several days later an article appeared in the area newspaper about a double murder in the area of Drover, Ohio. Citizens were concerned because there was possibly a killer among them. The fear took hold and drove the area to a state of alert and speculation. No killer was ever identified, and no other body was ever found. The direct deposits continued to flow into the account Paul had set up. Paul was never seen nor heard from again. His wife would only say to their children, "I don't know why he left us, but he left us (set for life).

Decades later a young deer hunter chose to conceal himself in a clump of extremely thick vegetation. As he crawled in he noticed a few scattered, gnawed bones. He kicked them aside and thought to himself that some animal had feasted on a deer carcass at some point. He never noticed the human skull deeper into the vegetation. Paul had left his family set for life, it couldn't be his life, but it was theirs.

Want

Needing to have and keep some dream
Wanting to share my dream to the needy
Opportunity knocked so I opened its door
A knock of success turned to life's failure
I got what I wanted - but what did I need
Who really knocked at the door that day?

Getting what I wanted not what I needed
Was a laughable granting by evil sources
Quick to provide a want - at regret's price
Sorry for a want - meant for some good
Expecting good to follow good is naive
Sadness lurks about - striking at our good

Sadness from good makes blind spots
Blind spots are entrances to weakness
In weakness - want auctions off need
Auctioned need - is purchased failure
Gaining a want won't guarantee a need
Know a want from a need and get both

Justifiable

Mr Pith Irvin was a gentleman, a poor man, but still a gentle man. He loved a peaceful atmosphere; tranquility was innate to his soul. He had bought a small farm, and came up with the idea to raise beef as a business. He would take a client to the auction, and advise them of which beef calf to purchase. He would take the calf to his farm to raise. The owners of the calf could visit their future freezer stock at anytime, and watch it grow. The work would be done by Pith for an extravagant monthly payment for pampered beef.

Pith was so pleased with the success of his venture, that he began to plan an opening of a butcher shop, an elite butcher shop. Customers belonging to his gourmet beef club, could have cuts ordered to personal request. Each customer had their own storage area in the facility, and could request a cut to be hand delivered anytime of the day or night. Pith worked the off hours for deliveries. He began to get acquainted with many influential individuals in the community. So successful was the venture that Pith made plans to open an "Elite Club", a very exclusive club.

A warehouse had been sectioned off into small quarters, each section was a very plush quarter, with a membership only admittance, this became the club. The cost of membership reflected the extravagances offered by the quarters to members fortunate enough to gain membership. Discreteness, privacy, chef prepared meals (Conventional American Cuisine), and a very professional drinkmaster, with the most complete drink selection imaginable. What Pith had created was a wonderland for women and men that could afford it, and had impeccable reputations. No matter what their true habits or lifestyles were, the public recognized them as they appeared, the respected and monetarily successful of society. Pith felt he could take advantage of them, as they had their communities.

Pith Irvin thrived in the environment, he truly enjoyed creating a club that was truly desired by any member, that didn't have a membership. To belong to the Pith Irvin's "Chambers" (the name of his very elite club) was to belong to the nearest semblance of aristocracy the area had to offer. With such limited membership, it was a sought after membership. So desirable that the pillars of society began to court Pith's acquaintance and friendship. Pith was offered tickets to the most exclusive events in the area. He saw that no other club could hold a candle to his enterprise. He was courted by politicians, members and officials of law enforcement, and well heeled individuals, both male and female. So successful was he that he began to plan for a resort on his land where he kept and cared for the livestock. That development would take much more money and time, but time is what Pith had, and the money was growing rapidly.

Pith was having a conversation one day about politics and the law. He had many questions concerning Grand Juries. How were they picked, and why were they secret? One seasoned politician who had been, and was still trying to ingratiate himself with Pith, told him that one had to be a very special individual to be on a Grand Jury. Although they are supposed to be picked like any juror, by summons, they were special. Somehow only "important" people were able to sit on a Grand Jury. He told Pith he couldn't explain that part to him, but if he wanted, he'd see that Pith got to sit on a Grand Jury. This excited Pith to no end, he accepted the offer immediately.

Sure enough Pith was called to serve on a Grand Jury. The case concerned the shooting of an unarmed individual by a police officer that said he believed the person was reaching for a weapon, and felt in fear of bodily harm. Pith had heard this so many times over the years, and had wondered just when would the nonsense end. Pith wondered to himself, just how many times does an officer have to fire a round into an individual before the fear of bodily harm ends. Yet each time these incidents occurred Pith had heard on the news or read in a newspaper, that the killing was found justifiable. He wondered what the Grand Juries were being told that the public wasn't being told. Pith vowed to himself, that this time it would be a rational and fair judgement, at least by him.

After the second day of hearings, Pith thought that the police officer in question was about to be indicted for sure, at least in his mind. When they were dismissed for the day, Pith was going to his car on the third level of the indoor parking garage when two shadowy figures appeared just outside the elevator. The garage lights made it impossible for Pith to see the faces of the men. Because the figures blended in with the night sky outside of the parking garage. One spoke, saying "The department can take care of you and yours". Pith looked confused and replied "What department". The voice said "You'll know, because when you look out for the department, the department can list you and yours among those that are known as very favorable to it". Pith asked again, "What department", but the figures disappeared back into the shadows, leaving only silence and a confused Pith behind.

Pith experienced a sleepless night. The next morning before reporting for Grand Jury Duty, he asked the friend who made it possible for him to be summoned, to meet him for coffee. Pith told him what had happened in the parking garage, and the friend didn't seem surprised at all, only nodding his head. This doesn't bother you? Pith asked in a slightly indignant and questioning manner, do you know what they meant by the "Department" Pith inquired. His friend spoke and said to Pith in a soft but knowing way, "Your wife has been caught drinking and driving, you have a son that's doing drugs and sometimes selling them, your daughter is running an escort service for some of your club members, male and female, and she's making a very good living, am I correct Pith", "Yes" Pith replied. "Well", said his friend, "I know this and the police know it too". Then his friend inferred, that the police can continue to look the other way, or bring hell to his life, and finished by saying "It's up to you." He told Pith that if the police felt indebted to him, they would go beyond the limits of the law for him, but they need him to know what his life can or can't be. "If they know that they have your support now, your life can be comfortably looked after by them, if needed", the friend said. Pith looked down, sighed loudly, and slowly walked out of the coffee shop.

Two days later an article in the daily newspaper read POLICE OFFICER FOUND BY GRAND JURY TO HAVE ACTED APPROPRIATELY IN THE SHOOTING OF THE UNARMED INDIVIDUAL, AND WAS FOUND TO BE REASONABLY IN FEAR OF BODILY HARM WHEN HE FIRED HIS WEAPON.

Pith looked at himself in the mirror after reading the headline, and saw a bought and paid for nobody. He couldn't respect himself, nor could he ever expect anyone else would if they knew his truth. Though no one needed to know that he had been bought, he knew, and that was one too many knowing the truth of Pith. He believed he had worked hard for his family, to bring good things into their lives. Pith believed that his love for his family and his protecting their reputations had taken all he had worked for, leaving him without dreams or purpose. Pith later that year liquidate all of his assets, to cash, left his wife and family and was never heard of by anyone again who had known him when he was happy and in love with his life. Pith never knew love again, because he had traded his self worth, the part of him where love grew.

Living and Dying

Full of life - living for all loves of mine
Working for loves - loves deserve life
Life in me - and giving them all of me
Me enjoying - giving them all my joy
Joys of building - is joy I provide them
My life is full - because they have it all

What is all - is all too much to possess
Did all - leave them enjoying nothing
Is nothing here - when all is in a home

Can home live - if a home has nothing
Where is the strength - if nothing holds
I'm not honored - by my loves of my life

I had me - until I gave me for my joys
Success was mine - but it had no truth
Truth was mine - until society be a liar
No longer me - no longer society's bee
No more do I live - nothing to be part of
Dying inside - nothing left outside of me

I'm somebody - being nowhere at all

The Older I Get

Perk was an old man that never really became excited about much in life, in fact his children didn't believe he was even excitable. Yet his children loved and respected his opinions on most issues. Each time they believed they brought special news, they would look at him with the hope of seeing some form of excitement in his eyes or some type of response. His calm demeanor was the same with the best of news or the saddest of announcements. From the birth of a new grandchild to the death of a family member, Perk could be counted on to bring reason and stability to most situations. One child decided to investigate his consistent demeanor and try to discover the origin of Perk's approach of calmness to almost everything he had encountered in his life.

The child began by making a list of relatives, still living, going as far back in Perk's life as he could go. He soon discovered that it seemed to be a pattern of behavior of those of Perk's generation or older, the same behavior of appearing to have a calm demeanor no matter what is going on around them. As though they had to appear to maintain the same calm temperament, no matter the situation. A behavior of making sense of everything going on around them. A first cousin of Perk agreed to talk with the child, and when the child had completed this interview, he believed he knew all he needed to know about his father. He gathered the other children and grandchildren one afternoon and revealed his findings to them all.

The child stood in front on the other offsprings of Perk and told them how Perk had been shot and left for dead at the age of fourteen, and had been the only member of his immediate family to escape a house fire at the age of twelve. After being left alone in life he had been placed in foster home after foster home until he was old enough to join the military. During his time in the military he was nearly lynched in the south for giving a man a severe beating, after the man had used a racial slur against him.

Perk had gone on to seek a profession and raise a family in a middle class environment. Through all of his calm demeanor, he had been a kind and gentle person, and very loving to his family members. Always eager to assist in anyway needed. But nothing was done in an excitable way.

One particular piece of information the child obtained was Perk's experience in the military, and when his parachute had only partially opened. Perk believed he had seen the other side and, knew there was life after this life, and that it had much more to offer in goodness than this life ever could. So it seemed that Perk was just living and loving until his time here was done. He believed nothing here in this life was worth being excited about, except leaving it.

I'm So Old

No longer can I be amazed because my fascination is now old
My fascination has been teased and tickled until nothing is new
What fascinates many is only a rerun to me - in word and pictures
Words that have aged my hearing until I can no longer hear some
Pictures have aged my eyes until I can't see others newly performed

I've aged to the point where I find it hard to find anything really new
Newness has aged my heart until the very newest is only old to me
Surprise has aged my mind until it says "Oh no not again" too often
Reaching for stars has aged my touch until I know they're not real
Realness has aged my being until I believe nothing is as advertised

I've touched the world until touching it has left blisters uncountable
The world has touched me until I age to not wanting its touch at all
The sinking lights of the world have aged me to know they blind me
This world aged me to know that white is really black, and has been
I've aged until I know that what I see isn't what I truly know is real

The new shall become the smell of the old repugnant vapors known
I have age to the point of what smells new to youth is ancient to me
Age has taught me that all is ancient, just painted differently for ages
The smell of no performance is the sweet smell of the truth we need
To the aged, the smell of need is the most painful, over a smell of want

I've aged to the point where the lies are the most bitter when told in love
Aged to the point that I know the taste of love is tasting understanding
Passion isn't love nor is infatuation or lust, aging I know it's only peace
Tasting peace with all that surrounds me is my reward for aging wisely
Aging soundly shall take me to the end of my time with a sweet taste

Nowhere To Go

Maturity is finding truth and peace in life
Finding what is real truth and peace -
Depends on one's starting point at birth
One, society will promise and deliver it
The other, only promises to promise

Mature resentment grows from doubt
Words encouraged trust and belief -
Depends on one's parents at birth
One society will assist as it is needed
The other only assisted as forced

Mature vision allows us to see our truth
Knowing peace, truth, and assistance
Depends on one's differences from some
One knows peace, truth, and assistance
The other only knows of the three visions

Ardis on Armon

Grandpa was the only name his grandchildren, Rufus, Zoe, Jordi and Zella used to communicate with him. Grandpa took questions from the young ones often, and more than once did the subject of monsters come up. Most assuredly the question of "Are they for real" got into the conversation. Most often grandpa would just say they're just figments of an entertainers' imaginations. The children accepted the half hearted explanation, but still seemed to carry some doubt in their inquisitive minds, expressed by the "Oh well, if that's the best you can do" expression on their little faces. As a matter of fact grandpa thought to himself "Is that the best I can do?"

When grandpa was rearing his own children, he and his wife Dorothy really didn't feel comfortable censoring entertainment. Their children David the oldest enjoyed monster movies from a young age watching them with his dad, who had reared David along with his mother until he married Dorothy and they had three additional children, Diana, Donna and Derrick. Diana also enjoyed the monster movies, Donna avoided them, and Derrick didn't seem interested one way or the other. These attitudes of the children seem to explain their own offsprings' interest or non interest in monster movies. Grandpa had been told as a child that these monsters in movies were not real, but that didn't stop grandpa, the boy, from seeing them everywhere in his room at night time, when he should have been sleeping. In retrospect and in present tense grandpa wondered just how did all these ideas of monsters begin, from where did they originate. Grandpa had been told by his mother and grandmother, as a boy, "Every story has some basis in truth.". Nowhere had grandpa ever heard or seen any evidence of the origin of these characters that carry the monsters' roots.

An idea dawned on grandpa one day and he looked forward to the next time the grandchildren asked him "Grandpa are monsters for real?". Grandpa could say with some certainty that the stories of monsters had true origins in the history of the world. It had become so clear to him after reading The Book of Enoch. So now grandpa could refer to the Book of Enoch in references.

Grandpa's opportunity to add some clarity to the world of his grandchildren came one weekend while he was sitting with them. The first question came and he was prepared for it as never before, heck he may even sing the explanations to the children, he thought to himself. The first question was asked, "Grandpa where did cannibals come from?". Grandpa spoke

----

Samyaza: of the unholy two hundred

Samyaza and his unholy two hundred descended on the world
Taking man's comely daughters and producing giants galore
Giants demanding and consuming all man could then produce
A production that became non sufficient to sustain the giants then
The giants turned to eating man and then consuming creatures...

****

So, grandpa said to the children, you can see how stories began. My grandmother and mother told me, "There is usually some truth in every story" When things seem a bit impossible to believe, ask yourself how such a story started, then search for its root.

Another child spoke and asked "How did primitive man go from sticks to weapons of war, even adorning themselves with colors to go into battle and to their women with seductive makeup. Grandpa spoke

"Every story has some truth, please remember that everything has an origin." Grandpa spoke.

Azazyel

Azazyel with the secrets of Heaven
Taught man to make weapons of war
And war.
Swords, knives, shields, Breastplates
For war
Taught making of mirrors, bracelets
Ornaments for the altering of man
Altering the world
Use of paints, dyes, valuable stones
Altering the world
A world altered by war
Man altered by vanity and greed

****

Okay grandpa, one of the children spoke up with a challenging look on her face, "What about magic?". I've told you children before and I repeat myself again, every story has a beginning, and a origin I tell you. Grandpa spoke.

Amazarac

Amazarac with the secrets of Heaven
Brought to an ever so ignorant world

Sorcery and the dividing shares of roots
To mesmerize and control ignorant man

Armers

Armers with the secrets of Heaven
Taught ignorant man to sorcery
But fight sorcery with sorcery was how
Ignorant man was mesmerized and controlled
                    Samyaza
Taught sorcery also

****

So there you have your spells and counterspells children. Witches and wizards, both have an origin in human history. Behind every story there seems to always be some truth. People may lose the original story, but some part of it seems to always remain.

Grandpa, one child asked, where did astrology signs come from ? How did something in the sky determine what people do, and predict things? Yes children even astrology signs have an ancient origin, grandpa spoke.

Barkayal

Barkayal with the secrets of Heaven
Predicted behavior and events of the stars
To ignorant earthly man
Ignorant man saw and tried to copy
What was only known in Heaven

Ignorant man tried but couldn't duplicate
Only try and talk about the secrets

***

There you have it children, man was impressed but impressed only. What was known in Heaven was allowed, but not the ability to do was shown to them. There's always truth within every story, always. You must search.

Grandpa, another child asked, how did the constellations in the sky get to be known to man? The same as every other Heavenly issue that exist in this world today, answered grandpa. Nothing has been invented by man, only observed and told about and expanded verbally. Grandpa spoke.

Akibeel

Akibeel with the secrets of Heaven
Taught placement and places of stars
As they were and as they should be
Man was impressed and remembered
And carried forth what he didn't know

***

Man shall alway say what he saw and doesn't understand but knows that he saw something he couldn't understand. So impressed by what he couldn't understand, it became a story to last through the ages. A story changed and altered, but from a beginning was a truth.

Well grandpa, how did man learn about the movement of objects in the sky, space, the universe, all from the ground. Again grandpa spoke firmly to the children, correct, how could ignorant man know the predictable movements of celestial bodies in our universe? Everything has a starting point. Grandpa spoke.

Tamiel

Tamiel with the secrets of Heaven taught man
Where a Heavenly body should be and when
Ignorant man was in awe of such knowledge
He could see but not explain the predictability
So he made stories to explain the universe
And passed the stories to his children and they -
Theirs

***

One thing predictable about man is that, if he doesn't have an explanation he'll invent one and call it the truth. Though it may require altering from time to time, the story will have some basis in truth.

Grandpa, how did man know the motion or phases of the moon so long ago when man was new? Like all else, things start with some truth and then the truths are expanded verbally, overtime. The phases of the moon are no different. Grandpa spoke.

Asaradel

Asaradel with the secrets of Heaven
Taught ignorant man phases of the moon
Man was impressed with such ability

That he told his sons and his sons' sons
Until it became man's "knowledge"
Even though he didn't know the workings
Of why and how

***

Nothing man can imagine is new, only new to a new man. Man lives and relives; alters and again alters his world to adjust it to his truths, or what he calls the truth.

Grandpa is asked how someone came up with the idea of vampires, you know, sucking blood and all? Children nothing is new, only altered because the origin has been lost to some extent, and only bits and pieces remain. Grandpa spoke.

Watchers

Watchers and Man's women begat giants
The giants began to devour men because
Man couldn't support their hunger needs
Then the giants injured beast of all kinds
To eat their flesh and drink their blood
Ignorant man wisely called out to Heaven

***

I say to each of you, my grandchildren, never scoff only suspect, then seek. This is the world of the watchers. There is much to be known concerning all that you wonder about. So I say to you at this moment, trust your foundation of the world as it is revealed in the Holy Bible, then there is much to build on, as you will learn if you seek.

The Book of Enoch is a frightening book, but only frightening if you don't have the foundation of the Holy Bible as your reference. Much information is found in The Book of Enoch, that can provide needed understanding.

As grandpa walked away he overheard one of the children exclaim "How did he get so smart.". Grandpa thought to himself "I hope smart grows into wise as they get older.".

"Wait grandpa", he heard one of the children say, "What about Zombies?". That's probably the clearest of all, grandpa said. Matthew 27:52-53, When Christ died on the Cross the veil of the temple was torn in two from top to bottom;and the earth quaked and the rocks split, and the graves were opened; and many bodies of the saints who had fallen asleep were raised; and coming out of their graves after His resurrection, they went into the holy city and appeared to many.

As I said, there's some truth in all stories: Grandpa turned and walked away.

Passing Through

The small brown stranger is ever so present in all phases of society, always happening to be there, anywhere. Often those observing him, see him as many a different being. He may come off as just a good guy, a nice guy, a sexy guy, or even an angry or vengeful guy. He may be seen as someone only the beholder can describe. But the beholder is the force determining what appears before them. The truth in an individual molds what appears to them. What a person professes is not always an indicator of the true individual. What is in the heart of the person is what's exported to him and he appears as what that person happens to be.

Most individuals in the society we inhabit in this "So- called" democracy, which is anything but a democracy, See themselves as good. How dangerous it would be for the majority to constantly determine the course of a society. It would assume the majority would consider the needs of the minority or minorities, not just themselves. We are able to point to several instances in history where the majority took its society down a less than pleasant path. Enter the Constitutional Republic, a set of rules, and three branches equal in our government, the laws of the society are made, interpreted and carried out by the three equal and separate branches, each a specific responsibility; therefore the majority can never steamroll over the few.

In such a society it is seen as patriotic to observe and respect the laws, and if necessary, to defend them to one's death. In doing so one should be politically correct, respecting and avoiding offensive interactions with fellow citizens. Enter the guised politically correct individual. The individual that has limited or no respect for a certain group of people in the society. Feeling that those people have no rights which they are bound to respect. But publicly professing equality for all in society. Emerging from the world of being politically correct is the individual resenting the decency of politically correctness, because the person doesn't possess the desire to wish all in society to be equal, and has harbored the anger until it became fashionable to rebel against being politically correct. That person in an atmosphere of rejecting respect for some in the society proclaims it unnecessary. In doing so that person can determine what offends another, relieving others of the responsibility to choose what offends them. There is a group in society that truly believes what a Constitutional Republic demands. They are the conscience of our society, the pride of our society, they are our Constitutional Republic guards of honor.

Phil sits alone in his bedroom at three o'clock in the morning, a Saturday morning. He wonders where it had all gone wrong. He had attended one of the most prestigious university in the land. He used his alumni connections to fulfil his dream of becoming a successful businessman. His business took him to great heights of admiration in his community. He was well respected and loved by most in his community that he was encouraged to run for political office. Political and business success were unprecedented within his family or high school.

Usually he was accompanied by his lovely wife and two well mannered children. Very active was Phil in his church, and insisted that his family pursue the same path, and become prominent within the Christian church. Phil was a scout leader. He tried to instilled the goal in his son, of someday becoming a survival expert, as he had done in his youth. He had attempted to give his daughter clear goals, marrying up or laterally, reaching a prominent position in the community, by using all of the family contacts, alumni from her educational background from an elite university. His wife was everything he wanted, attractive, according to entertainment's version of attractive, supportive and well respected within the community.

His wife had been molded into a shape foreign to her truth, and still existed in that mold. Somewhat resentful for being what he wanted her to be rather than what she could be, she remains loyal to the ship but not the captain; she had other desires of independence attempting to surface. In childhood and teens she had chosen to ignore her attraction to those of the same sex, but in irritation from being dominated so long, it became an outlet in need for her independence. Unfortunately her attraction led to her involvement with husband's assistant of many years. Finally she had some sense of independence from him, sporadic as it was. One day the assistant suggested they make a life together, away from him. The wife thought for some time and replied, "This will take some time to Process", but they did and then carried it out.

The Son did become a survival expert, and later a convicted child molester. The daughter did marry up into society, when she married a female entertainment star.

It's three o'clock one Saturday morning, and Phil sits in his bedroom on the side of his bed. He looks out the window and sees a small brown stranger looking back at him from across the street, who turns and walks away when Phil makes eye contact with him. Phil sits alone in his bedroom at three o'clock in the morning, a Saturday morning.

In his political career, but less so in his business career, he used as a cornerstone, the Constitution of the United States for a standard for respect. It seemed to some as though he didn't intend, or ever made it clear whether he meant the Constitution applied to all in the land. He made very clear his expectations and entitlements of it.

There are Small Brown Strangers among us, only passing through, who know and feel the truth dwelling within us all. What is the purpose of him knowing what he sees, feels and hears going on inside of you, if he has no idea. All he knows is the truth registers with him and when you look him in the eye, you are aware of his knowing your truth. A smile won't, a word won't, a gesture won't disguise what is inside of you! The Small Brown Strangers walk among us daily until they are full and can no longer bear the weight of the walk, so they retreat knowing the truth of society until they feel strong enough to rejoin society.

The Small Brown Strangers don't know why the weight of society goes away, but it does each time they retreat. During that time little by little the burden lessens. It may take days or weeks, but they do refresh.

Those in society see them as their Small Brown Stranger, but the stranger they see is reflecting what is their truth within. Rather than wondering why some less than pleasant, appreciated or joyful event has taken to them, they may want to examine within, and try to make clear their being. Vanquishing or welcoming the invader or invaders of their existence is what determines what they'll see, the next time a Small Brown Stranger passes through. They'll hopefully see a more tranquil small brown stranger, depending on their choices of love versus hate.

A Gathering Point

Small brown eyes gather truths in places
Gathering honesty for why they know not
So many eyes so many places in a point
The gathering feed where they know not

They lack knowing what they do or feed
Simply seeing places and those in them
Only knowing what pain or pleasure exist
In places they have to pass through daily

Some truths bring joy or lightheartedness
Others bring a weight curving their backs
A need to retreat for lessening of a load
Weight bearing truths require real purging

Channeling weight of proportionate size
Back to its origin of conception to dwell

In the mind that is unaccounted for in us
Good for good - sorrow for sorrow it is ?

The brown stranger just passing through
Knows not what he sends or what returns
Only knowing their pleasure and pain
For being what is - in a world that is

Resulting

Donny was an outgoing person but an equal amounts of energy searching within himself for answers to questions he had as to whether there were truly any limits on what he was capable of being or doing. He acted out these same concerns when interacting with others on many levels, personal and general interactions, while also trying to see the truth in others. It seemed to him, even as far back as childhood, these concerns were present and active within him.

Donny often thought of the days when he lived in the Lee Seville Projects of Cleveland, Ohio, known as Miles Heights. In the years he spent there as a child, it seemed that each summer included an appearance by a three quarter ton truck pulling a huge compressor that emitted a thick white fog as it drove through all living areas of the Projects and the vegetation areas around them. The projects were surrounded by wooded areas and even some swampy areas, where he and other children played pirates on makeshift rafts. The swampy area was located behind the local dump. Where he and his friends would search the cracks and crevices of upholstered furniture, looking for coins that may have been left there when the piece was discarded.

Donny's brother David built his first bicycle from parts obtained from the dump. Donny loved looking at old things people threw away and also catching snakes in the dump area with his best friend Johnny. He and Johnny would become lifelong best friends, they would serve in the 82nd Airborne Division together and never lose touch through senior years.

When the truck with the compressor would come each summer the children, mostly the boys, would follow it while it circled and made its way through and around the Project area. Some of the boys, mainly Donny and Johnny, would enter the fog emitted and see who could remain in the fog the longest period of time. The winner, of sorts, would always seem to be Donny. While others, except for Johnny, coughed and choked and ran out of the fog, he seemed to be quite comfortable and relaxed as he watched the others flee the fog. Donny would stroll out, feeling somewhat energized. In later years Donny came to realize he had been inhaling DDT insecticide, which was legal in the early nineteen fifties.

Donny's naivety was exposed when a childhood friend and neighbor pretended to eat a type of sumac that grows in the North East Ohio, and told Donny it was Indian Candy. Donny spent the next several years nibbling on the seeds of the red cone shaped clusters and telling other kids that it was Indian candy. The somewhat sweet taste of the cone, at least to Donny, seemed to leave him feeling somewhat energized.

The cold icy winters of the North East Ohio were beautiful, but also limited in the amount of time a child could spend outside at play. The boys in the neighborhood at times would grab hold to the back bumpers of cars as they passed, and let the cars pull them down the snowy and icy slick streets. One day as Donny ran behind a car to grab hold of the bumper, his feet slipped out from under him, and he saw his feet outlined against the sky as he landed on the back of his head and neck. He had no idea where he drifted off to for the moment, but it was a place of euphoria. Suddenly he realized that he must be on his back in the in the street, he began to remember his feet outlined against the sky and the impact on his neck and back of his head. Donny got to his feet and looked around to gain orientation. At that moment all seemed serene and peaceful, and once again as in previous experiences he felt somewhat energized.

Through the remainder of his childhood and into his teens, Donny began to notice with increasing frequency that he was aware of moods and intentions of those that he came in close contact with, or just in close proximity when passing on the street. One incident in particular demonstrated the ability to be very real.

During his time in the military, while serving with the 82nd Airborne division, Donny was asked to testify against a Sergeant in favor of a PFC, Donny was an E4 at the time. Some time after that, a demonstration parachute jump was scheduled for foreign dignitaries. Usually for demonstration jumps, machine gunners and rocket launcher gunners were allowed to stuff the GP (General Purpose) bag that normally held a machine gun or rocket launcher, but for demonstration jumps, were stuffed with a sleeping bag. These were known as Hollywood Jumps. The sergeant against whom Donny had testified stated that he would pack Donny's GP bag. When Donny lifted his bag and looked into the eyes of the sergeant who had packed it, he knew that the sergeant was attempting to kill him. Yet on the other hand Donny just smiled to himself and thought "Today is not the day.".

On the plane the men jumping with the GP bags usually stood in the door and exited first on either side of the ship. On this occasion the same sergeant, who was the jumpmaster, pulled Donny from the door and told him to exit last. Donny Complied with the command. When the last jumper on the stick on Donny's side left the plane, he struggled to the door with his exceptionally heavy bag and exited, using all the strength he could muster. When his parachute opened, he found himself in a violent spinning motion and the GP bag still attached at the upper webbing; but the leg strap had come undone and the bag was straight out in front of him as he spun clockwise.

Donny fought against the spinning by trying to somehow force his Risers counter clockwise. Risers are used to guide the parachute. He wanted to stop his clockwise spinning by encouraging his Risers counter clockwise. He watched as his spinning continued to get closer and closer to the canopy of his parachute. He thought to himself "If this continues it will eventually close my chute (parachute). The spinning finally stopped as the ground approached. He used the releases from his webbing, with much difficulty, and let the bag drop from the webbing of the parachute harness. Then it hung by the strap still attached to the webbing, hanging below him. When he had landed and had his

assistant gunner Max, assist him in carrying the Bag from the drop
zone, he opened it, and what Donny found inside were wooden ammo
(ammunition) boxes filled with sand.

Donny surmised that when the sergeant pulled him from the door,
he had released the leg strap, held in place by a quick release that
snapped behind his leg. That would have kept the bag close to his body,
and not become an object caught in the wind of the propellers (Prop
Blast) of the C-130 Hercules aircraft. After returning to Company
Quarters, Donny was walking behind the sergeant and directed his
thoughts toward him and expressed something strange. His thoughts
told the sergeant "I know you tried to kill me for testifying in favor of
the PFC, but I knew it wasn't going to be today! But what I do know
today is that you'll die in a war". The VietNam war had not become
well known at that time in nineteen sixty three. The sergeant turned
toward Donny with a terrified look on his face, but immediately looked
down and headed for his quarters

Decades later Donny visited the VietNam memorial and saw the
sergeant's name on the Wall. The sergeants choice was written on his
wall of fate the day he chose to attempt to kill an innocent man. Donny's
naivety and innate innocence was admired by some and exploited by
some, but the innocence and naivety seemed to be his defense against
all that would do him physical or mental harm. His lack of interest
in petty life situations, such as who likes him or who doesn't, had no
place his thoughts. Only Life's big picture, compassion and truth was
of consequence to Donny.

Donny physically intercepted attempts of bullying of friends when
he was young. Being able to recognize true intentions in the words of
others caused him to jump in verbally and a time or two physically,
when others suffered verbal or physical intimidation, at least those who
seemed weak and or meek.

He had no tolerance for arrogance, to him those individuals had
no place in his personal life and he gave no time or thought to them.
His personal growth thoughts were mostly spiritual. The more time he
gave to spiritual growth the stronger religion became in his spirituality
(Christianity).

While getting mail from his mailbox one day, he turned to go back to his door and found he was being charged by two ferocious Staffordshire Terrier (Pit Bulls) dogs. He wore no shirt when he went to the mailbox, and all he had on his upper body was his Green Scapular, in honor of his patron saint, Saint Paul. Donny was baptized in his name. He related his late in life conversion to Catholicism to that of Saint Paul's conversion to Christianity, and besides, Donny's middle name was Paul. As the dogs charged, growling and barking, he happen to look down to his chest and gaze at the Green Scapular, he held it in his right hand, and somehow knew he would be unhurt. One dog veered off to Donny's right and went towards the street while the other stood in front of him and growled then just turned and walked away. Donny gave the situation much thought, and wondered just what did the two dogs see that turned them away. He did know for sure something had interceded, and surely it was a force of protection and good.

Donny's ability to sense truth in others, whether it be good, bad or evil, was a great asset in his career as a Registered Nurse for more than forty years, almost always. He knew immediately how to interact with any individual. No matter how pleasant or distasteful the interaction happened to be. The same was true in his social and personal life. It was a gift that he didn't understand, but was well appreciated by him.

Words coming from the mouths of many people, are not the words of their heart. He realized he shared his life with them all, on some level, and who was he to judge the heart of others. Donny's heart and hands were busy making himself into the man he thought would be attractive on Judgement Day, the best a bride may ever look, is on a wedding day, that's how he wanted to look on his Judgement Day to Christ our Lord and Savior, He Who will Judge.

Whether it was standing in the fog of the insecticide, eating the "Indian Candy, or the blow to the back of his head and neck during a fall, or a combination of all these events, Donny doesn't attempt to figure out what makes him so aware. He is just thankful for what he was given by Goodness, and he should never abuse it by judging what he believes dwells within others. The gift of knowing the heart of another is to know how he should answer a knock at the door of his life, to open the door or let the door remain closed

Testament to Superiority

Vile and corrupt ways may now be foreign to me
Directed hate and gossip I choose no longer to be
All things putrid and foul smelling belongs to thee
Your's were slavery, and forget not wounded knee

Vileness encouraged corruption I left for the dead
Corrupt and cruel are stereotypes you did spread
Fear of equality caused you restlessness in bed
Lies become your truths this is how you have led
You in league with the fallen is all that can be said

Gossip filled hate grown and exported all around
No home or love for us can in this world be found
Hated for fighting chains and our chest we pound
Absent your fallen league nothing said is so sound
Let your vanity and ill will make you so hell bound

Rather than compete - trodden are just held back
With fallen ones influence you have the inside track
We not in line get a place to fall through - the crack
Deplored in public - praised and admired in the sack
Fallen's influence won't let you accept what you lack

Lies become truths and lies become all you are now
Lacking an integrity of a horse pulling a farmer's plow
A horse is what it is and not selling what is left by a cow

On equal footing you wonder what can be done now
So you take greatness of ours and display it as a sow

You be you and I'll go on being me -
I know who I am - from me I don't flee
Making me wonder who is truly free

Eureka

Bright eyes, is what his mother used to call him, and Mrs. Williams, his best friend's mother living next door, used to say "Don't buck your eyes at me.", always with a smile. So many little girls used to ask him to be their boyfriend, before he even knew how such a situation worked or evolved. In school, he saw teachers sending a smile in his direction when he looked up from his paper or book to give more thought to his assignment. Boys his age and some even older wanted him to participate on their team when choosing sides for play. Male adults around the neighborhood would see him and sometimes say, "What are you up to today?", always with a smile.

He felt so free when he could just run or climb a tree. He loved the thought of animal behavior, watching the ones he could observe on his own. Within himself he was always competing and trying to do things better than he had done before. A constant competition within his body and mind. Honesty was so innate to him that he believed it existed in everyone. He was so trusting, that he believed all to be the same as he, existing in a personal world of honesty. Deception was not a part of him, his mother had even told his new bride "If you want to know the truth just ask him.".

No matter what others saw in him, he only saw an average boy, teen, or man, depending on what point he happened to be in his life. As a child he only wanted to be the best he could be, as a teen he had his own goals, not ones influenced by other individuals other individual. More often than not he was living within himself, occasionally stepping out during the day to interact with whom or what was appropriate at the time of day or place where he happened to be. He was adept at being alone in a group or in a one on one situation. Often his thoughts and verbal responses to conversation during interaction diverged greatly, depending on how much effort he felt the discussion deserved. If some saw it as arrogance, he only saw it as life, after observing his own growth for a lifetime.

He was attracted to the opposite sex, but only courted those that courted him. He always felt unworthy of the attentions of those considered, attractive according to the world of entertainment's version of female attractiveness. This was his behavior as an adult also. Until one day a woman with whom he had a relationship made the comment "You can have any woman you want.". The statement bewildered him for a long time; he wondered how she could ever come to that conclusion.

As times changed and women became more outspoken, and less concerned about being what some called "of proper morality", which in fact had handcuffed women to subservience in his opinion. Women had been programmed to a place of obedience and for chattel. Women began to approach him openly and aggressively, seeking his attentions, and after a period of time he learned to accept their wishes and desires, and eventually he learned to abandon waiting for their attention and openly sought their advances. In doing so he became so successful at gaining attention of females, that he was the poster boy for the term "sexually promiscuous man". A title he neither applauded nor condemned. It was just life according to him, kind of a development in his mind.

Many women spoke out against his behavior to co workers or acquaintances, but secretly endorsing, fantasized, or seeking out his attention. If not him then those having similar behaviors. It continued until he felt as if he hadn't learned anything, just another person living what they want and not what they are.

A time came when his new world was only a world of beautiful people being beautiful. They didn't seem to be about anything, just skin deep, with nothing else to offer. Previous relationships he had been engaged in were involved thought by both parties, before the so called beautiful people "women", found him. Behaviors of substance, and advancement of mind and body. To him a stagnant person was a dead person, entombed in a life of sameness, minus growth of thought and awareness. They existed in the sameness two, ten, twenty years later. They presented the same thoughts with the same voice and inflexion.

He was able to find beauty where he looked for beauty, his kind of beauty, existing in mind, body and soul of those abandoning blindness and nothingness.

In leaving behind what some may call "worldly beauty", he had only one thought and that is "I didn't look for you; you found me and I didn't like what you found in me".

Found and Lost

Surprised was I to find you standing there
Stark worldly beauty nothing else to spare
Staring because the thought I didn't share
I didn't know this where is your only where

Before me you stood stating your own view
Never having heard it from others like you
My self image became what is truly askew
With what you give to me what can I truly do

All you are is standing in front of me - now
So taken back am I - thinking I should bow
Trusting your words - to them I should vow
This given freely - all the sweat of my brow

I could have any woman I wanted you said
Words were so foreign to words in my head
That place not visited by me you well read
Your place is a tiresome place of the dead

You took me to the only place you can go
A vast wasteland where nothing can grow
There's no rivers there to freely live or flow
Skin deep with skin deep - nothing below
I walk my way now - you've lost your glow

The eyes have it - beauty found
Skin isn't forever - wrinkle bound
In checking time - the clock be wound

Now I understand

Respected and looked upon favorably by most, those not approving of his place of authority are noticeably silent, only speaking with looks of contempt. Words they apply to his authority or place are non committal. His close friends and acquaintances in the workplace make him feel warm and in touch with co workers. Things go so well, even the presence of those disapproving for any number of reasons, are kept in constant check, there is no opening for character assassination, which was prominent in the world of choosing sides in this workplace. To get in good with the influential in the administration, some wished well due to loyalty, likeability, or convenience of a stepping stone. All had personal reason, to justify their positions held in that workplace.

With life and every instance in this world, things change, sometimes for the better but too often better is not the case. When changes occur in the workplace it does affect more than the obvious individuals. When management changes so do supervisory positions, resulting in changes in loyalty of previous supporters of said supervisors. For instance, an expressed lack of confidence in their decision making that was formerly praised. Those once thought of as close co - workers are then openly defiant and critical of the supervisor. Those that had been less than supportive are now smug and arrogant, leaving that supervisor to have learned a great lesson in life and in the workplace. The only true supporters of those displaying honesty and fairness are God our Father, and in most cases, our parents.

Now That I See You

We met so long ago but this is my first time seeing you
The smiles - warm and supportive conversations had
Our agreements of what should and should not be true
Pledges of future trust and bonds that had taken place

To me - you now look like a stranger that had no loyalty
One that sees me as an outcast - never to be friended
Your words offered to me are of indignation or disrespect
Where was this you - when we walked common ground ?
Am I new to you or a case of me never really knowing ?

Your back is turned more than you appear to face me
Am I now grotesque, unusable, or no longer interesting ?
One left in your place is cruelty that was absent in you
Or was the person I see now just sleeping or festering ?
The person you reject now - you rejected always within ?

Were pledges and treaty one sided - living only in me ?
I didn't see - or maybe chose not to - of my dear friend
A trust that is blind - a pledge in blood is a life promise
Did the one I know die and this one assume his place ?
If a pledge is for life - yea your life passed from pledges

A future gone and bonds were broken the day he came
Building businesses raising families lost in a transition
One that took you and left another to break and enter
So long stranger and goodbye to my friend - two gone
One left living in his understanding of truth !!!

Nothing to do

Saturday night and no plans for the evening. The same Saturday night for the past several months. Lost touch with his friends, no active relationship with the opposite sex. Nothing in that area had changed for the past several months. Now it was Saturday night, and nothing interested him in television programing as far as he could tell. Tonight was an especially restless night, a night that would not let him just sit and stare mindlessly at the television until he was too tired to stay awake. Tonight he thought to himself, "I'll just go down to the corner bar and have a drink. He took a quick shower and put on some fairly decent clothes from his limited wardrobe. He took a spontaneous glimpse of himself as he past the full length hallway mirror. Not great, but presentable he thought. As he closed the door behind him, he gave a once over to his neat little home, and thought to himself, "well, I like it neat even if no one else sees it". He got into his new car, backed out of his driveway and headed down the street to the corner bar.

He could hear the music coming from the open side door. Good music he thought to himself. When he entered the bar, the smell of cigarette smoke and alcohol in the air was kind of appealing to his senses. The men in the bar were loud talking, and smiling individuals. Everybody held drinks of all sorts in their hands, or drinks sat on the bar near them. The women there were dressed somewhat revealing of skin, and they all had smiles on their faces. He hadn't had a date or a relationship in months. For that matter he hadn't seriously sought one. His female co workers were all dressed properly for their employment, pants suits or skirts with a matching jacket. Never revealing anything other than face, neck, hands, and portions of legs, appropriate portions, he always thought to himself. They seemed to do nothing for his sense of sexual attraction. To him they were just his equal; with sameness and predictability, efficiency and dependability. He often thought to himself that they were too much like him to be attractive, maybe because he wasn't attractive to himself for some reason at this uncommitted point in his life.

He ordered a drink as soon as he found an open seat at the bar. The bartender was a middle aged good looking woman. Very attractive, yet not revealing any skin other than face, hands, and legs from the knee down. The front of her neck was exposed, the back of her neck was inside a turned up white collar. He found her very attractive. He wondered to himself if it was the boyish short haircut, but no, some of his female co workers wore short boyish haircuts. Ahh he thought, it must be the perfume. The fragrance was almost intoxicating to him. She served his drink with a smile and a slight wink, he nodded his head in return. The bartender went on, tending to her business behind the bar.

He sat and savored the warmth of the alcohol mixture moving down his esophagus to his stomach where alcohol is absorbed. He had a second drink and a third, and was just enjoying the atmosphere of the surroundings, the music, and the people, the combination of odors in the air. It was a combination of alcohol, cigarette smoke, perfume, men's cologne, and sweat from those engaged in dancing. He hadn't felt so relaxed and tranquil in such a long time that the feeling was almost foreign to him. He got off of his bar seat and walked towards the jukebox. He stood there and scanned the choices on the screen. As he scanned the screen a voice spoke softly near him saying "Play D4" He looked to his side and saw a middle aged woman that reminded him of the women he worked with, except she wore bright intriguing makeup and a low cut blouse; the fragrance emanating from her engulfed him in pleasure.

She wore a skirt that outlined the lower half of her body perfectly, because it seemed to be a perfectly built body. He was in somewhat of a trance, broken by her suggestion that they dance to "D4". It was an oldie, one that was sultry and passionate. She was a very smooth dancer, while he was only adequate on the dance floor. They danced to a couple of more numbers and then as he started to head back to the bar. She suggested they take a booth while it was available.

They slid into the booth one from each side and were able to face each other. She seemed to find him just as attractive as he did her. They talked for a while about very superficial events, until he asked her where she lived. She smiled a coy little smile and said "On the other side of the fence in your backyard.". He looked very surprised and she just smiled. He noticed how her eyes sparkled, just like one of the women he worked with each day. She told him how she had watched him from her kitchen window often, and she noticed there was no woman in his life. He asked about her marital status. Uninvolved, and not married, she replied.

She told him how the choices she made in relationships never seemed to end up in friendship to say the least. Although at times she had hoped for more, right now she wasn't looking. She said she felt comfortable approaching him because she knew a little about him, a least where he lived and some of his behavior. She added that he looked different than most men in the bar, behaved differently and appeared conspicuously lonely this night. He just nodded his head and added "Well said, well diagnosed.". You're so right he thought, nothing that I can add to that, and then said it.

He said that he knew where she lived, what she drank, her kind of music, and that she was an excellent dancer, but nothing else. Her response to his statement threw him off for just a second when she suggested they get to know each other better. His words left no doubt about his being in complete agreement. "Let's drink to that", the two of them happen to say in unison as they held their glasses up to toast. Both of them lowered their heads and shook their heads while smiling broadly, because of the way they both were thinking the same thing (let's drink to that). They then sipped from their drinks and leaned back and both took a deep breath. Where do we go from here he thought, and then said it. "I'm not sure, going out to have a drink has kind of already happened", she replied.

She was suggesting dinner and a movie, when he injected "How about going fishing" He said he knew of a few farm ponds and small lakes where he had caught a few Largemouth Bass and he said if that's not enough, he would take her to the place where ducks walk on fish. "What, ducks walk on fish ?" she asked, "Yep" he replied, "it really happens". She said "where is this place" ? He said "it's in Linesville, Pennsylvania, about twenty miles from where we'll be fishing if you choose to join me". "Well, you certainly have my interest and I'm definitely going to take you up on that trip".

After they had agreed to meet at her home the next Saturday morning, they both thought it would be fun to talk across the fence when not talking on the phone. The next five work days wouldn't pass fast enough for him. She was on his mind the whole work week. He couldn't get over how some of the women he worked with reminded him of his new acquaintance. It made him give them more smiles during the day, instead of a head nod and a slight grunt.

Saturday morning arrived and he was ready, the anticipated weekend had finally arrived. He had his fishing gear in the trunk of his car, and he was dressed casually, but very neat. He pulled into her driveway. She came to the side door and asked if he would like to come in for a beer before they went fishing. But he was too excited and wanted to get started. He loved fishing and was happy to have a possible fishing partner in tow.

They took the scenic route through the suburbs of Cleveland, into rural North East Ohio. It was what he thought was possibly the most picturesque time of the year. They visited a few friends that he had known when he lived there, and introduced her to them before they allowed him access to their farm ponds. The fishing was just as he said it would be, but what he hadn't said was that he was a firm believer in catch and release.

She soon realized he truly respected all animals, in fact he respected all life. She really admired that in him, particularly when he stopped his car, got out and pushed a turtle off the road with a stick. He told her that he pushed it instead of picking it up was because it was a snapping turtle and it could take a finger off with one bite.

They spent many more weekends together, and a few nights. One evening while discussing work, they realized that they worked in the same complex. He knew by now she meant more to him than any woman he had ever known. Their conversations became more involved, even discussing what they would do with two homes in the same neighborhood. They discussed the pros and cons of selling or renting one, in either case, which one. Their time together, once they were both home from work, was dedicated to each other. He suggested that on Friday at the end of the day she meet him in his office and they'll head out camping and hiking for the weekend from work. She agreed by saying, "great idea". They arranged the time and place of their meeting, and said goodnight. This night each spent in their own home.

The week passed and friday at the end of the day he looked out of his office door and watched the elevator, which was quite a distance from his office, looking to see each time it stopped to see if she walking out of it. He waited and waited. After what seemed like an hour the door opened and he saw a woman inside dressed very appropriately for work, only face, hands exposed, and her suit with the proper length skirt showing a proper amount of lower extremities. She stood erect, very little makeup if any could be detected. He thought to himself, "What a woman, the epitome of sameness, efficiency, dependability, and predictability. I don't believe I'd ever meet her in a bar, but it wouldn't be the worse happening in my life, in fact I would welcome it", he thought to himself, then whispered it quietly.

He waited and waited, the elevator came and went, with the same woman on it. He wondered if the woman that remained on the elevator was trying to get up enough nerve to say something to him. Finally, sadly he decided to call it a day and go home to his nothing to do life. He put on his coat, walked slowly to the elevator. Pushed the down button, and walked in when it arrived. It seemed to him, the same woman was on the elevator, or at least her twin, was standing at the rear. It seemed somewhat eerie to him that she had some facial features similar to the woman he was waiting for, but this woman looked too reserved and stiff to be anything like her, at least at a quick glance. The judgement he had just made was made with one quick look. He had just turned his back to face the elevator door, when he heard a low sultry voice say "Play D4".

Blinded By the Sight

I couldn't see what I wanted to see
What I was looking for lay beneath
Look on water's reflective surface
Tells nothing of what is underneath
Beneath swims the needs for many

Shall we paddle along only on top
Never seeking our treasures below
Surfaces show wrappers on a gift
Wrappers indicate a probable good
Leaving the prize to be found inside

Looking past you as I looked for you
Unable to see below a calm surface
No sign of the current moving things
That provide necessities and desires
Things that give our lives substance

Often we navigate life seeing its top
How can we see what supports life
Good life or not the foundation tells
What supports is so rarely displayed
Supports are what determines a life

First I had to know foundations of me
And know what I've had from the start
Looking below your surface I see gold
You provide my reality and my dream
On a calm surface and a current below

The Right Time

He was a wanderer that didn't know what his potential was at the time. He mostly did whatever was fluid at the moment. He didn't give much thought to tomorrow, and most yesterdays were days of regret for choices made without much deep thought. Though he was definitely capable of deep thought. He pondered situations of the world and their solutions in his pre teen, and teen years. In one area was so lacking that it led to most of his in appropriate decisions, in the area of personal relationships, male or female. He found most male acquaintances to be boastful and disingenuous, and women were a total mystery to him. He also further complicated his social interactions by being extremely shy. He later understood his shyness was due mainly to his lack of understanding of the opposite sex.

He, a hard worker, was very successful at making and maintaining relationships with co workers and management. He felt at ease in the presence of any of them. No sense of shyness raised its ugly head at any point, that is not until the owner's secretary appeared in the work area from time to time for any number of multitude of reasons or just for a cup of coffee. He discovered at some point he's not sure exactly when, but alcohol consumption relieved most anxiety he felt during female interactions. He was a relaxed dancer, and held a comfortable conversation with women, as long as he was under the influence of alcohol.

One Friday evening before getting off from work, a male friend suggested they hang out together that night in his area of Cleveland.

He agreed to meet the guy at his apartment and they would leave from there. He's not sure who suggested it first, he or his friend, but they did "Get a jug", meaning let's get some alcohol to drink. After drinking some in the car, his friend said that he knew a girl that was just right for him. He had consumed enough alcohol to say that he'd like to meet her. They went to the woman's apartment, and the friend introduced them to each other. She was a small woman, very attractive, who held an intelligent conversation. He did notice that she enjoyed drinking as much as he and his friend. The friend watched the two of them dance to different tunes, and converse on a number of issues, appropriate, and not so appropriate for two adults meeting for the first time, but that's the way it went that night.

The subject of food came up, but they agreed they all had drank too much to drive to a restaurant. His work friend said that he knew a little store within walking distance where he could buy something, but he wasn't a very good cook when he was drinking. The woman volunteered to do the cooking if the two of them went to buy the food. They went and returned with the making of a meal and more alcohol. She cooked the meal, and the three enjoyed her cooking. After they had finished their meal, he danced with her some more, while the friend sat and nodded off to sleep. She suggested that he not drive all the way home at such a late hour, after having so much to drink. She invited him to spend the night. She woke the friend and suggested he go home, since he lived nearby. He yawned and stretched and said "See you folks tomorrow."

It was a very passionate, sensual night. When they woke the next morning so did his shyness, to his surprise, she seemed just as shy. They had difficulty looking each other in the eye, and they made conversation that was purely superficial. She made the offer and asked him if he would like a morning drink. A morning drink was new to him, but he accepted the offer, and the transformation took place. They both returned to their night before personalities. They talked about anything coming to mind, even spending another night, which he quickly agreed to doing.

The relationship became one of alcohol love and alcohol induced companionship. Eventually they moved in together. He gave up his apartment. When he wasn't at work and was at home with her, everything was secondary to drinking. Friends visiting brought alcohol with them or the new couple supplied it to them. Without the drinking there was no foundation for the couple being together. The couple seemed to accept that fact, and it went on for more than a year.

One evening while they were entertaining guests, an old boyfriend of her's showed up at her door. She allowed him to come in and she introduced him to her new mate. All seemed cordial, but the old boyfriend began to visit more frequently, and he found out later the boyfriend was visiting her while he was at work. After long conversation she admitted her old boyfriend had told her that if she went back to him he would rejoin the military and guarantee her a monthly income. She said she told her ex boyfriend or (soon to be again boyfriend) that she wouldn't accept his offer if her new mate would marry her. He, her new boyfriend, felt the ultimatum was forcing him into something he was not at all interested in doing.

It turned out to be what he thought it to be, the right happening at the right time. They separated he went back to college, and became a professional with no love for alcohol induced conversations. He happen to see her in downtown Cleveland one afternoon. She was leaving court for some infraction, she wouldn't say the type of violation. The beauty was gone, the intelligent conversation was non existent, and she still smelled of alcohol. As he walked away from her he couldn't help but think, had he not walked away that day, he would be walking with her now.

The whole situation taught him that he should only depend on his own intellect for interactions with anyone, and to do whatever possible to gain greater intellect. Most importantly he learned shyness is a state of mind feeding on fear of interactions of some type, and to banish the fear he must confront it. He found it helpful to be more honest with himself when interacting with the opposite sex.

When he thought of how the woman he knew for that period depended on alcohol just as he did, he decided that all people are shy, it's just that most overcome it in one way or another. His way was to confront it directly. He asks himself even now, what was there to be so apprehensive about. Women are just people with different parts, but the same brain in many ways. He now realizes that alcohol doesn't change reality, it only delays it.

Only Anxiety

Only anxiety can make caution my fear
Or make my simple - easily complicated
It can turn my smile into a face of terror
Sadly I run when I should stand at times
Choking my words instead of allowing flow
It makes me stumble when I should glide

Anxiety isn't knowing what I should know
To look and not turn away and to speak -
When it tries to bind my tongue my lips
I should dance with it and not freeze up
I can touch it to see if it's as hot as it looks
I can live anxiety or touch it and know it
Knowing is to understand - not folding in fear

A Little Silly A Little Angry

Feeling a little silly and a little angry
At managing my fears and phobias -
By ways of living fears and phobias
Not realizing what I was really living
Living faith in evil - not living in God

Superstitions are worldly teachings
Exaggerations of life's exceptions

Believing that we can control it is -
Ignorant beliefs we are gods within
We can lessen evil by choices in life
Our Heavenly prayers can banish it

What Now

He had been married for thirty years when cancer made him a widower. Gone was the camaraderie, friendship, competitor, ally, foe, advisor, medic, confidante, student, accountant, and admirer. Little did he realize until she was gone what it took to be his spouse. For so many years she was just there doing what she did, being all of those things to him and all the while being a mother to his children. So spectacular was she in retrospect that he found himself knowing the anchor of the family had been lost in this sea of life, during one of its storms, leaving him adrift.

He would think back to the days when they first met and see her in her youth again, so vibrant, so full of ideas and plans for a future, a relentless builder of sequences of happiness, not the cancer ravaged body lying in that hospital bed before him. The voice she had responded with for thirty years and the four years prior to their marriage, no longer responded. He remembered her last words to him "What time is it?", he responded "Ten minutes to two". Little did he know that would be their last verbal interaction, because when she slept after that moment she never woke to speak to him again.

The two of them had lived their lives within each other and among the lives of their children. It seemed that the two of them were the only ones recognizing the ills and the good, along with the hopes of society and world. They had an unspoken language for communicating in a group, signaling approval or not of subject matter. They seemed to be so equal in so many ways, inferior to each other in others. They trusted each other implicitly but each guarded defiantly against any sign of dominance from the other.

Now that he was alone he thought to himself," What a wonderful relationship we had". He stood alone at that point, everywhere they had stood together in their courtship and marriage. He wondered if one that was two could ever be a complete one by himself. It seemed to him once he took inventory of their lives together, he had delegated so much to her and just out and out depended on her. Trying to put things in perspective he thought out loud, "What now?"

Their children showed true concern for his well being, but they had lives of their own. He believed as the father his responsibility was to continue to give counsel and nurture them as well as he could, the way she had always done their entire lives. The pain he felt had to be stored for when he was alone, to allow the children to express and navigate their loss which was the biggest they had known to that point in their lives. He could only hear their distress, and reinforce the wonderfulness of what she had given them as long as they could remember, by reminding them of what she left with them rather than what she took with her, and what she took with her was only herself. What she left behind were children that were compassionate, honest, and hardworking. Things they couldn't buy in this world, she gave freely out of devotion and love for her family. What his family had and what she left the family was all well and appreciated. Standing alone in their house, they had made a home, he reiterated his previous thought to himself and voiced softly, "What now?".

He began to wonder who and what he was without her presence. Their lives had been so wrapped up in each other and in the lives of their offspring, they had left little room for outside interest if it didn't involve both of them. The loneliness grew, and he had little interest in anything outside of having a drink at bedtime. The bedtime drink turned into afternoon, then morning indulgence. Months passed and and he began to appear emaciated and gaunt. All the while less able to tolerate food consumption. His gait became unsteady and weak. His son offered different types of foods, but he found food unpalatable. His day turned into one of staying awake long enough to continue drinking.

He seemed to have chosen to do this until he could joined his spouse in death. He thought to himself, "What now, is there in life for me?".

There was much left in life for him coming down life's road. He attended a church Mass with his son and seemed to wake up from the indulgence of despair. His interest in Christianity's understanding, and being a Christian grew by leaps and bounds. His interest in prayer grew and seemed to give more understanding of Christianity. His view of the world was clarified along with his understanding of non adherence to Christian ways by those proclaiming to be Christians. Dedicated to Christianity he felt an obligation to do what he could to advance Christianity. He took to writing in hope that his beliefs and views of the commandments of Christ would endure when he no longer lived in this world. That's what now could be.

Coming down life's road also was a relationship like one he hadn't known. It was one of giving and receiving, while understanding the importance of both. The biggest gift of the relationship was that, he'd found love again. Someone to share and enjoy life with on a level different from any he'd known before. This new relationship led him to write about respecting people and being charitable to those less fortunate than him. His sense of charity, and ability to engage in charitable deeds grew. Along with everything else which opened up to him he gained a sense of responsibility to identify ills and hypocrisy in society. That's what's now, and always.

How much we don't know about what waits down life's road is an issue to be lived, and not speculated upon in despair. When we believe life has nothing left for us, we're bowing to death and giving up on living. Only Heaven knows what's down our road, and what it will mean to us and others. It's our choice to live it or die without it. He went on to live the healthiest he'd ever lived, feeling loved and in a state of mind where he wanted to be what Christianity is, and has been, and will be no matter what distortions some attempt. True Christianity is pure, It's flaws are those with non Christian agendas. What now is everyday.

It's a Challenge

When life is good evil wants to know -
How shall I put grief and pain therein
Can I proceed to life's next station or -
Shall I lay and waste away to naught
A choice of mine vying against death

It's easy to dance when it's my music
I'll sing along when I know the words
Dance and song lead to smiles within
When I smile within I can glow outside

I think of grief and pain, and wonder -
About my virility during confrontation
I know what I believe it shouldn't be
A confrontation of weaknesses despair

Walking into and out of grief and pain
Is not a walk of joy or one I anticipate
But a walk that's made by all for sure
Grief and pain is life's constant visitor

Despair's oppression is ever increased
Leave me helpless and not fit for fight
Only in a position for me to succumb
Even more than my moments before

I choose to proceed to find what is
My life waiting for me down the road
Not rollover and be what despair is
Rushing to nothingness unprepared

Tight Lipped

His role in the relationship had gone from speaking up and giving an independent viewpoint to avoiding confrontation by averting conversations from becoming major issues, when they were of no consequence to either of them. He began to believe she had found a way to frustrate him, which led to anger, which in turn caused him to become less rational in what he said. She would gloat whenever he reached that level in their arguments. He truly thought it was a form of control on her part, that she used whenever she felt neglected and wanted to punish him. He came to think of it as a form of discipline on her part. He decided to remain uncommitted to specific responses to her points in conversation that he thought she was using as a segue to confrontation. He learned to hold his emotions in check by not exposing them to unwanted exploitation.

So successful was his new approach, that he saw a change in her behavior. Each time he thought she was about to urge confrontation he'd give an uncommitted generic response to her verbal stimuli. When antagonism failed she seemed to be somewhat confused by his response, or better said, opaque response. In time, silence became her bid for attention. He found her to be more attractive and approachable when she was less verbal. Because of his behavior of being non confrontational and argumentative, and her subsequent response to his new behavior, she became less of a tempter torch, and more a recipient of his attentions. Happily ever after?

It turned out she wasn't so fond of his new attentions and the way he delivered them to her, and she rejected them. He found rejection unbearable; and soon in turn found her unbearable. They were able to part on good terms and wish each other well.

What Happened

I thought you'd like the way I look
When I was there looking upon you
I didn't expect to live your rejection
Nor embrace you pushing me away
Nothing left to hold nor wish to hold
We agree to say goodbye - now go
Two misses

I tried to be what you wanted me to be
That made me who you didn't want
I made a move it moved you away
You lost that feeling of "us" being us
Too bad

I did need to change to keep us "us"
A change wasn't what was needed
An understanding of us was needed
I didn't know it then - but now I do
Too late

I didn't expect or want your rejection
That changed who you were to me
Your change made you undesirable
But you had no wish to be desirable
To me

Now we frown and now we do walk
Away as two strangers former friends
Two extremes from one commonality
Unable to adjust to familiarity together
Two gone

A Day and A Night In 1971

It was getting close to summer vacation, and I'd taken most of my finals, so I decided to take the afternoon off from classes. I just drove around for awhile until I happened to pass a lounge I'd visited a couple of years before. I took a seat at the bar and started to scan the jukebox offerings. I sipped my drink while enjoying the records that I had chosen. It was a warm sunny day. The kind of day that could make anyone feel in good spirits. People came and went in the establishment, while I just enjoyed my fantasies, and tapping my foot to the beat of the music.

As late afternoon approached, a young woman entered the club and took a seat next to me though there were several other seats available. She wore the shortest skirt I'd ever seen. She was as attractive as any woman I had ever met. She was very petite, a wisp of a thing that bounced around as though she possessed endless energy. She didn't seem to have any reservations about invading my personal space. It didn't upset me at all, in fact it pleased me quite well. Her leg bumped mine and I made some lame remark about hot legs (from a Rod Stewart song). It was the best ice breaker, or come on, I could think of on the spur of the moment. She turned to me and smiled, such a beautiful perfect smile, and we began a conversation that lasted for hours. She said she was from Montreal and we talked about everything while we continued to sit at the bar.

Finally I thought I'd better get home, because I did have studying which needed to be done. I didn't want to leave but I just had to bite the bullet and go. She said she'd like to see me again and I told her I wouldn't be able to see her until the weekend. She told me to call her if I wanted to see her again and she wrote her phone number on a piece of paper and handed it to me. I looked at it, and up until that moment, I hadn't realized I didn't know her name. On the piece of paper above the telephone number was the name Mina.

I attended classes and did my studying the rest of the week, while she continuously occupied her claimed space in my mind. I thought of her energy, her smile, and of course, the short skirt and wondered what the weekend had in store for me. Whatever it was I surely planned to find out. I was quite taken with her, given the short time of knowing her, but the fact was, I seemed infatuated, mesmerized, or just plain in a haze. To this day I can't say exactly what had happened to me. My feelings made the weekend seem so far away.

The morning of the weekend arrived, and I was up before daybreak planning my attire for the evening. I'd never been efficient at matching clothes, but this day I gave it my best effort. After trying several combinations, I finally settled on what I would wear for the evening. I washed my car until I it sparkled. As the day passed, the anxiety of the slow moving clock often challenged my patients. Finally evening came, and I picked up the phone and called her. She expressed pleasure that I had called but did say she wondered why I waited all day. After we expressed mutual extreme pleasure for our first and only meeting, we decided it was time for me to go to her house. She gave me the address and then she told me to hurry.

I pulled into her driveway, took a deep breath, got out of my car and walked to the front door. She answered the door in the most alluring negligee I could have ever imagined, and at her side was the largest, most intimidating, but beautiful German Shepherd dog I'd seen in many years, and I know dogs. I had worked with German Shepherds and Doberman pinschers when I was in High school at a dog kennel where I attended shows with the owner. The dog was very well trained. After being introduced to me he took his place in the living room and just monitored me, the guest, as a well trained dog should. She offered me a seat on the sofa where we both sat with drinks she had prepared and took up our conversation where we had left off when we were last together.

Talking led to physical activity and she suggested we retired to the bedroom. When we stood up to go into the bedroom so did Atlas, her dog. (I thought it a very appropriate name for a dog that size). She told Atlas to "Stay", and as I said before, he was very well trained. It was a passionate night that went into the morning.

We had coffee and talked a lot. When I was about to leave I noticed suitcases in one of the rooms and I asked her if she was going somewhere, and she replied yes.

She then went to a briefcase opened it and took out a roll of United States and Canadian currency, a roll she held with both hands. She said she was going to Pittsburgh from Cleveland and she would give to me half of everything she had in her hands if I went with her. I gave it very serious thought, but it meant leaving Nursing School for uncertainty, well financed uncertainty, but still uncertainty. I told her I couldn't leave school, but I was attracted to her and would have liked to be with her, but not at the cost of leaving school. She said that she was leaving that day. I looked at her and saw all she was in my eyes. I regretted saying I couldn't go, and words of a changed mind stayed hidden.

It was only one day and one night out of thousands in my life, but hardly a day has passed I haven't seen her in her negligee, walking in the bar, standing at the jukebox in the short skirt, introducing me to Atlas. I wonder if she ever thinks about me.

I've Got Moments to Remember

There are moments to remember and some to regret
The few you gave me are some of the best ones yet
I don't know if there's a name for feelings we had
Remembrances are feelings of happiness and sad

No wish we'd never met - in stone feelings were set
We can't say love - we didn't incur that kind of debt

Still feeling you - so it was and wasn't a one nighter
Sharing happiness I had with you but only as a writer

The ups and downs in my life and you're always up
One day and one night was wine from a golden cup
Few gave such joy - such unbridled living for now
I can't say I did it again since you - I don't know how

What we lived is stored in my life's memory bank
Having what we had for a short time is life's prank
Wishing it was longer - is a penny lost in the well
We know what is - what would've been I can't tell

Remembering is my reward in our case I believe
Living life at your pace would be truly ill conceived
One thing is true - I don't regret our day and night
Freedom I learned - living reserved is living fright

Run Away

He was well traveled and most would've thought him interesting. Interesting he was not, merely a man soaked in failure and inadequacy. He traveled often, because he was often running away, away from possible failure and being revealed as having nothing of substance within his personality. In the wake of his life's choices lay a myriad of self destructive decisions and potential abilities left standing untouched.

It seemed he never really recognized the good opportunities staring him in the face, at the time they were revealed. Another of his deficiencies was taking most individuals at their word. He wasn't one to deceive or misuse another's trust. He usually recognized too late another individual's absence of honor or trust. Often he found himself dumbfounded when he discovered someone had misled or misused him. Yet he never really seemed to learn a lesson from any of the incidents he experienced involving misdeeds done to him by someone he trusted.

After years of failing to realize any potential he thought he had, whether real or imagined, he stopped making choices, all but one. For many years he avoided contact with those important in his life because he didn't want them to know his weaknesses and failures. In real terms, he'd run away. He disappeared from family and friends for weeks or even years at a time. Returning even more of a failure, which then led him to run away again before settling in on his return. Running away was his lifestyle, a very unusual lifestyle, but it was his. He never had any substantial accomplishment to show for his twenty five years. No sustained relationships developed by a one time outgoing and fun loving highly sociable person.

One would have thought he might continue the same traits he displayed as a child. When his family moved from the neighborhood he felt so comfortable living in, his personality changed. He was a new teenager, thirteen years old, in an environment where friendships had been established for years, just as they had been where he previously lived. His social abilities and intelligence allowed him to exist on the fringes of many groups in his new environment. He was never the pillar of any group. He could associate with the Children in the college prep sections in school, though he was in the business course. He also mingled with the neighborhood tough kids, the science minded kids, and the kids with no direction at all, or so they seemed to him.

Now as an adult he was still living on the fringes of life. With his intelligence level, one would think he'd be at a much higher level for employment opportunities. Yet it seemed he was just a job drifter, which went well with his run away lifestyle. If there were signs of his advancing on a job, he would make a choice to remove the chance.

He had returned to Cleveland one weekend, and decided to call one friend, who had been his friend since he was four or five years of age. His friend suggested they meet. When they got together, his best and only friend looked at him and asked, "What happened to you"? He had tried to dress somewhat presentable, but evidently he'd failed. He got home that night and walked past his mirror and got a clear look at what his friend saw. He thought to himself, "That's it, things have got to change for me and I'm going to change them.".

He started by finding work, no matter if it was at the bottom of the work ladder, he was going to become the personable, sociable, and outgoing individual he had been prior to moving to a new neighborhood. He was a dependable employee. He encouraged himself to be gregarious, and intentionally become intimately involved, whenever appropriate with co workers and new friends. He even found himself enjoying the person he had been at one time. He chose to go back to school to seek a profession, and excelled in that profession when he graduated. He finally realized he had forgotten who he was and didn't know the person that replaced him in those empty years. Thanks to a friend, one willing to speak the truth in what he saw, he was able to live again, and not do what he had done for so many years, run away from living, and only exist in limbo until that life ceased to be livable.

He can look back in his life, and around him and see people that existed the way he had. He wonders if they'll find their answers the way he did. He knows it's a waste of time in a life to avoid living. All one has to do is remember who they really are, and call themselves back home, evicting squatters that so brazenly set up house in their temple.

Is Living

Is living being what I believe others -
Think I should be or even doing ?
Is living doing what I believe others -
Approve of me doing, be it good or bad ?
Is living give or take what I believe others -
Think I should be accepting or rejecting ?

I can do what I believe - not what others do - Trust
I'll be what is me - not what others want - Honor
I speak for me only - not what others speak - Belief
I'm walking my way - not what others walk - Steady

Please don't tell me what's good is bad - Evil
Or even that the darkness is really the light - Blind
Keep away the idea that cold is really warm - Empty
No truth in the idea tough is really tender - Pain

Living what I believe is living a hard way - Committed
I'm accepting or rejecting by my experiences - Living
I remove all lies being called truths - Quest
I look through my eyes to see others - Truth

Short, Long and Short

He googled her name, and to his surprise and sadness an obituary came up. He leaned back in his chair let out a long sigh and closed his eyes and started to remember. His thoughts went back to his younger days, much younger, when he'd only been discharged from the military for a matter of a few weeks. He had pulled up in front of a delicatessen store on East 140th street in Cleveland, Ohio in his 1961 Chevy convertible. There he saw a young woman that, simply put, made his heart leap out of his chest. He hadn't gotten out of his car yet, and they looked at each other through the windshield. She gave him a big smile and he smiled back and winked at her. She returned the wink, still smiling broadly. He felt there was nothing else to do but to strike up a conversation and hope it led to a relationship with her. He got out of his car and approached her, she was very receptive.

They became a couple, and seen as one by most of their friends. They were considered inseparable. Any time they were apart, was a miserable time for both. The dream relationship went on for months. They were like a couple who had been together for a long time. They were totally dedicated to each others happiness. Anytime he was seen in his convertible, she was next to him, with her big smile and beautiful brown eyes, very long natural eyelashes, and petite stature. To put it bluntly, she was a looker.

Things went along happily for the two until about seven months into the relationship when she told him she was pregnant. He was speechless, as her eyes filled with tears. Those beautiful brown eyes were now glassy with tears. She asked what they were going to do. He was as non committal as he could be. They didn't discuss it. They acted as though nothing was different other than her stomach starting to show her pregnancy. One day she hit him with a bombshell; since he wasn't going to marry her, she planned to move to New Orleans with her family, who were moving there anyway. He didn't address it, probably because he was numb. He couldn't imagine being without her. The days passed, until the day prior to her leaving. Their last day together was like a funeral, little spoken, and great suffering by both. When she left, it was as though a large part of him cease to exist, the part of him that could love.

He moved from one relationship to another, hoping to get the feeling he had with her, but never finding it. He began to believe it would never exist for him again. He went on year to year, learning to fake love, then faking love routinely, and easily. All the while she still remained prominent in his memory, and he saw her in his mind as she was the last time he stood in front of her. He believed he could honestly say, that a day in his life didn't pass without some thoughts of her. He wished he had been man enough to accept responsibility for what he had done. But that hadn't been the case, and he rarely spent a day without regretting what he had let pass him by. He wondered everything possible to wonder, when he wondered about her.

He liked to think that if he ever found her or got in touch with her, things would be just like they were before they parted. On occasions when he dreamed about her, he would experience deep emotional pain when he realized it was only a dream. It happened periodically over many, many years. He lived his life with her permanently placed in daily thought. How wonderful it would be, just to talk to her just once more.

One day he happened to see a name, and remembered that she had a sister with the same unusual name. He obtained the phone number, and called. He told her who he was, and she said she knew the name as the father of her sister's child. For a moment he wondered if she would assist him in getting her sister's phone number, but she readily did so. He thought to himself, what in the world will I say when she answers the phone.

He dialed the number and listened to the phone ring, with his heart pounding. The ringing stopped and a voice spoke, "Hello". He hesitated, it was her he thought. The voice was a little more mature, but it was definitely her. He spoke and said her name. She replied "Yes". He thought to himself, now's not the time to freeze up, he spoke," It's me" and said his name. When she replied, repeating his name, he could almost see her smiling. He said, yes it's me. It was the friendliest conversation he had had in years, maybe since he had the last one with her.

The conversation went so well, they agreed that he would visit her in New Orleans. Both were almost giddy about the possibility of seeing each other again. Arrangements were made and the day came for his flight. The plane landed and he walked from the gate to the terminal. They had both described what they would be wearing. Just as he entered the terminal area, he laid eyes on her for the first time in twenty eight years. They embraced and kissed as though they had never been apart. The reunion could not have been more enjoyable, for the both of them, so enjoyable that they planned to live together there in New Orleans. He went back to Cleveland and terminated his employment, settled other matters, then drove back to New Orleans with everything he needed to start a new life with an old friend.

When he arrived in the new environment the two of them sat at her kitchen table and began to plan the rest of their lives. Employment was no problem for him since he had very marketable skills, and she was already employed. Sadly though she told him his son, who had been born after she moved from Cleveland, was in prison in Louisiana, and was a frequent offender. Every family member of her's he met, commented on the the build, mannerisms, and looks he and his son shared. When they went to visit him in prison, he was amazed at how much his son did resembled him.

They reached a point where they settled into a routine of work and spending as much time together as possible. He enjoyed New Orleans French Quarters entertainment, and frequented the area. She on the other hand was used to it and wasn't as enthralled as he was.

Things were much fun for them; she taught him new recipes, cajun style, and he taught her landscaping and car maintenance. One evening at a bowling alley he noticed how she was attracted to the video gambling machines, while he was bowling. He didn't give it much thought until it was time to go, and he couldn't get her to leave, because he couldn't get her to stop gambling. On other occasions he noticed what he thought was a marked increase in her alcohol consumption, which had been increasing by the day.

One Saturday evening while they sat in the dark listening to oldies music, she poured her heart out to him. She told him what her life had been like as a single mother with all the challenges it presented, and what she had done and suffered in the process. The stories of her life as a young single mother brought on feelings of guilt, sadness, and shame in him. He had failed her, he thought to himself, by not stepping up so many years ago to a situation he helped to cause, and now all he could do was listen to what she had endured.

The guilt, sadness and shame made a change in him. He became less communicative and she complained about him not talking to her. His behavior grew more introverted, and she complained to the point of crying and begging him to talk to her. This went on for several weeks, until one night she put a gun to her head. She said if she was going to lose him again, she wanted to be dead. He made a rocking motion while sitting on the side of the bed, as though she was truly scaring him, until he could rock forward and turn the revolver away from her head, pinning her hand to the bed and taking the gun.

Selfishly he thought only of himself during the incident. What concerned him most was being found alone in house with a woman with a bullet in her head; in Louisiana, a place where no black man wanted to be charged with a crime. He took the gun and tried to think of a place to hide it until the next day. The next day would be enough because he wouldn't be there after tomorrow. He hid the revolver in the oven.

The next morning he didn't have much to say to her until she said that she may stay home from work that day. He encouraged her to go to work, saying that she would feel better if she did. She left for work, and he began packing his things. He gathers everything except pictures he felt his son might want, since he had no history of his father's side of the family. He drove back to Cleveland, regretting the past several months. He wondered, why he thought anyone would be the same person after so many years, he wasn't the same after all those years, or was he?

He went back to his life, hoping he was much wiser, but there were many reasons to think he wasn't. Some years later he sat at his computer and googled her name, and an obituary came up, and saw she had died at fifty six years of age. He googled his son's name and another obituary came up, his son had died on the same day of the year as the mother had died, seven years later.

He thinks to himself, we'd better give a great deal of thought to the choices we make in our daily life because no one knows where those choices may lead. He knows now he should have never treated life as a party or game. When the party is over, there's always a mess left behind, that may or may not be too big to clean up.

Fix It

I shouldn't have tried to fix old with old
It didn't work then and it doesn't work now
I should have let memories be just that -
Thoughts of pleasure visited sometimes
Why did I turn pleasure into a sadness
Pleasure thoughts gone forever since...

I can cradle a memory - hold it to my me
In remembrance of a pleasured past -
Sing to my memory songs it liked too
Because the song feeds the memory
Nourishing it within me, within its realm
Where it lives and only lives there...

We only live once reliving doesn't exist
Each moment is a life unto itself alone -

We can learn, making better moments
Ones without guilt, regret and shame
Let memories expire never revive a one
Memories resting in peace allow me to...

I'll recognize gone and past from now on
They're places I left moving elsewhere
To the next gone and the next past left
To move elsewhere to leave it behind -
I'll keep moving to the next gone or past
Until it's me that's gone and has passed...

I Believe I See It Now

I can't see how one can assume Heaven is their destiny. I believe Heaven is our heritage to be achieved, but we must be children of our Heavenly heritage. Everyone being a sinner, means to me, that it's a gift to try to live as Jesus Christ commanded. With the two commandments He gave us, we can imitate his life and can obtain what He promised, as best we can, considering that no one is without sin in this world today. He commanded us to put no one above His Father, and love one another as He loved us. His love for us is so strong, He gave His life, sacrificing His body and shed His blood in order for us to achieve our Heavenly heritage. Can we recognize that same love as Christ spoke of and demonstrate it within our hearts and behavior today? Based on this premise, can any one or any religion assume Heavenly heritage prior to Judgement Day, the day each one finds out what they have inherited.

Denying Heavenly heritage and Heaven is a license to indulge all of our worldly afflictions, and join the religion of science and the world, (the world being of evil influences) and working unceasingly to oppose The Laws of God and the commandments of The Christ.

What I believe I see now as the truth, is when He says He goes to prepare a place for us, it's a place in Heaven or a place not being Heaven. Since none of us are truly deserving of Heaven except saints chosen by Heaven. We must all realize, that the two commandments of Christ, are the only way to our heritage. We can't be blinded by sinful shortcuts telling us we've achieved Heaven before we die in this life. There will be Judgement when we leave this life and a final Judgement. Anyone professing otherwise is in conflict with Christ and Christianity.

We are obligated by His two commandments to place none above His Father, and we are also obligated as Christians to love each other, not discriminate or hate. Christ told us to Love one another as He loved us. How can behavior such as vanity of race, elitist position in society, self destructive cultural influences, ever fit into the category of loving others as He loved us. Until one can say he doesn't discriminate or live an entitled life, suffer from affluenza, or refuse to recognize the needy among us, he can't say he's on the road to a truly Christian way of life, and is imitating what Christ taught and obtaining what He promised.

Fear the Truth

In this case it's not wrong to fear the truth
The truth being very few shall see Heaven
Though we may not feel we deserve hell
Fear we are not good enough for Heaven

Peddling easy made up ways to Heaven
Grasping a theme saying we do achieve
Holding on to branches pointing to ease
World of sinning meant only to appease

Fallen ones knew good but chose it not
Having His teaching but we choose it not
Ignorance is nullified if a heart knew truth
How can we ignore sinfulness we choose

The world may make us want to lie or cheat
Cheating goodness and lying for this world
Hating for its sake is stone thrown from hell
Ask daily if we are good enough for Heaven

Denying God is worshipping evil incarnate
Dismissing Christ is welcoming hell into life
Incarnate evil and welcoming hell is a path
When we ignore Heaven's Commandments

Rama

He was homeless but managed to find a place to lay his head each night. Friends and family had lost trust in him, but they continued to have hope for him becoming the individual they all believed he could be. But this night he was locked out of the house where he rented a room by the week. He walked the streets and hoped he wouldn't draw the unwanted attention of night time predators or a zealous police officer. He had very little of monetary worth, but that would only anger a night time strong arm individual. He didn't have proper identification to show a police officer, so he feared that would start an unpleasant encounter with a patrol officer, protecting a community. The situation would have become more complex because he wasn't even a citizen of the community. He had come to this city because he was in hiding, potentially from the law, and from unlawful types for having taken revenge on one he felt deserved retaliation.

He was able to find employment through the Ohio Employment Bureau. He was personable and very intelligent, although his intelligence took second place to decision making when he was indulging in mind altering habits. The habits kept him living on the fringes of society, barely holding on at any given moment. But this time he was at his very lowest; no one to turn to, nowhere to go. There was no one he could call to help him as he had used up all the calls for help from those willing to give assistance previously.

Alone and sad, walking aimlessly he started to reflect and assess his life as it was now and what he hoped it could be. His first thought was how warm his childhood home had always seemed, and he thought how wonderful it would be to experience the feeling again. Next he looked at his current situation and sensed his own disgust at what he had become. He had become like someone he used to look at and wonder how they ended up in such poor condition. Unseemly garb, empty stare, and in desperate need of a haircut. He believed the only place to get a new start was to go home to Cleveland, where at least he felt comfortable and familiar with the area. But he couldn't go home yet, he didn't know whether he was wanted by the police for retaliation against someone who took advantage of him, or if that person was out looking for him. Being wanted by the police was his greatest concern. He almost wanted the person to confront him, hoping to finish what he started. That's no way to think he said to himself, that's not how to start a new life.

The night passed, and he went to the room he rented by the week and stretched out across the bed, and got some welcomed sleep. He didn't go to work that day and he didn't go out that evening. When he returned to work the day after, he intended to dedicate himself to work and get enough money to return home without having to have to ask others for help. With this new outlook, his mood seemed to elevate to a level he hadn't experienced in a while. It felt good to him to have some direction and purpose to his day to day activities.

The day came when he decided it was time to go home. He took a Greyhound bus home, and rented a room while he looked for work and an apartment. His heart pounded when a police officer stopped him for jaywalking. The officer asked him for identification, which he presented; an identification with a Cleveland address. He held his breath while the officer ran his name through the system. The officer returned his identification and handed him the ticket, and just told him to move along. There was no sign of the person with whom he had differences with, even after word of him being home had gotten around the area.

He stumbled upon a very good job the next day, after answering a want ad. The job paid very well and was close to public transportation, which was necessary until he bought a car. He met a very ambitious woman, who expected him to be as ambitious as she was. He played the part well, and began to enjoy the success that came with ambition. They moved in together, eventually married, started a family and he never looked back. He became what everyone thought he could have been the whole while he had been wasting his time being who he didn't want to be. He went from the lowly self destructive, self defeating, selflessness he had endured, to a lofty place in his mind which migrated to his entire being.

The Wrong Foot

Getting up on the wrong side of the bed
May lead to getting off on the wrong foot
The wrong side of the bed puts me weak
Waking in the morning let my caution be

A restless night gone leading to morning
Took me off my game to see clearly today
I ran when I should have walked to work
In a fit to do what I shouldn't want to do

Compromised views via the wrong foot
Views of one in a fit and not of standard
Made to order for one's reckless planning
Leaving me to live what I shouldn't live

Doing what I know I shouldn't, self defeat
A day of defeat is a day fallen far behind
Days of strength and courage to stand
It's harder to stand on any wrong foot

Waking up on the wrong side leave it there
Put a right foot on the floor and balance
Uncertainty in a life of my ordered chaos
Soberness and insight brings order home

His Shoes

He measured his mental health and well being by the condition of his shoes, at least that's how he interpreted his condition. His idea of the shoe blending with garb starting from the ground, meeting the socks or no socks, on occasions, to the melting of dress with his trousers or legs, if he happen to be wearing shorts. He wanted his shoes to reflect him as much as a shirt does. All of this went into evaluation of his psychological being just by looking at his shoes at a moment when he wanted to believe where he stood, as far as confidence and impressions radiated. If he was working hard, did his shoes say what he believed. He believed his shoes told his story, "now".

This morning he looked at his shoes as he lay across the bed with his feet over the edge. So appropriate he thought to himself, so appropriate. His shoes lacked any luster, they were very worn on the side and the soles were so thin, they were almost gone. The heels were worn to near a thirty degree angle, on bi lateral edges. The socks he wore weren't even matched, and the non cuffed trousers couldn't reach the shoes due to the absence of what was not available at the time they were obtained. He didn't have a belt to hold his pants up, but they were a little tight so it didn't matter much. His shirt was just a plain short sleeve solid color. His undershirt was grey, because he didn't care about washing anything, "now".

The day was gloomy, but oh how he wished the sun shined on him, but it wasn't to be today. He got up from his bed and paced the floor, and then stopped and looked out the window. It was a very grey day, it looked as though it might rain, but no rain so far. He watched the geese or ducks, whatever they were, flying south, or at least that's what he surmised. He tried to imagine objects in the sky from cloud formations. The wind made the trees sway, and tossed leaves about in the air. From his window he watched people come and go. All types of people on different missions he imagined, each had their own purpose. He thought to himself, I surely won't be going outside anytime soon, at least for, "now".

He heard a noise outside of his door, and he said with a smile and some sarcasm, "Room service". He took his food and walked to the stand. It wasn't the best food, but it was nourishing. He just picked at his food, then pushed it away, and walked to the door and looked both ways, but didn't see a soul, "now".

He retreated to his bed, and lay down with his forearm across his face, and thought about years gone by. He thought of how he was so meticulous about his dress, and of a wardrobe second to none. When he stepped out on a date he wanted the clothing to be a focus on him, at a meeting he wanted all admiration to be for him, or at a concert he wanted his entrance and attire to be about him; he felt he had to be immaculate all the time. He ended up in a heated argument, almost a fight, with another male individual over who was the best dressed at an event, and about whose outfit was more expensive. How silly he thought his behavior had been, "now".

He wondered to himself, how many people that cared about him, people he put second to his stylishness, stylishness of clothes, not of character, cared now. He hadn't heard from anyone, family or friend, because he left them in a pile just like he left his old clothes. Truthfully he didn't expect anyone to care about his condition. He never cared about theirs while he worshipped clothing. So he believes he understands, "now".

Everything he thinks about is about "now". There isn't anything else to think or care about except "now". "Now" is his whole world, what has been, what is, and what will be. "Now" is his world, a very sobering world. A world where all things are put into perspective. Priorities are

seen as should have beens, "now", which don't matter a bit, "now".
Because "now" is all he has, his last day on Death row is "now".

Worth

Contemplation is easy when I give myself time
Issues become concerns when I have time...
Smoldering embers within can become a blaze
Hot air may feed a flame taking it to the rooftops
When roofs burn and collapse all shall be lost

I seemingly lean towards a quick judgement
Often finding myself wishing to do it over again...
What's done is done and so it becomes the past
Prudent is to rethink or retreat to clearly assess
A best of all outcomes is truly at hand that way

What was big is so small in lament of reflection
I may find a fighting issue only a concern later...
Can I master converting mere big to simple little
Often bigs are nothings masquerading as primes
I must know what is and is not worth fighting for

Do I know why I may be susceptible to a fight
In what frame of mind did I enter the situation...
Was my mind being prepped for an altercation
I ask me if I was a fight looking for a happening
Maybe I was looking for a fight when I left home

I am an ember meeting a blow hard full of hot air -
A mixture for combustion - neither walked away...
Both roots of anger began before the encounter
Neither solved a problem - both fully regretted it all
Try to always walk in peace and humility to live

Trying Times

He promised to be faithful in the relationship again, just as he had many times before. The acts of infidelity were at a point where he had lost count, and some he didn't even remember, only surfacing occasionally in his memory. Everytime he said it wouldn't happen again, he meant every word, or so he told himself but it was just a matter of time before he was scolding himself again for his lack of fidelity. He was a good provider of necessities, but never had it in him to consider giving wholly of himself. Often he failed and often he promised better for the future. He tried each time he promised, but somewhere along the way his failing reappeared. He had a problem; he suffered suspicion in every relationship he'd had going back many years to a time when he was trusting. When he was betrayed by a best friend and a girlfriend, he could no longer be comfortable in a relationship. The fear of betrayal stalked the corners of his mind and no matter how much he promised and tried, the suspicion left him to think, "If I'm being cheated on, it'll happen both ways.".

Was his cheating an excuse or a defense mechanism? He didn't know, because his life of cheating had cascaded into a cycle of affairs, one night stands, and what he thought were relationships of love, that is until his paranoia surfaced and he began being unfaithful while being unfaithful. It may have been madness, but not to him. It had become how he lived his life. What to some would have been living in madness, was not to him. He survived in life, his way. How could it get any worse he thought, but he'd thought that before and it had gotten worse other times. Maybe he did or didn't realize his state, but he surely had to wonder why it continued to get worse and not better. Was something else feeding his condition he wondered at times.

He recognized that his experience of having someone be unfaithful to him, while he showered her with love, left him as an untrustworthy individual. That was one thing he thought, but was there anything else? One day at work he happened to listen in on discussion among female co workers. Though he had heard them talk before, he had never truly related what they said to his feelings about trust in his relationships. More and more he realized their words of admiration, fantasies, and infidelities outside of their relationships, ranged from braggadocious to a simple fact of life of their infidelities while in relationships. It seemed as though they were no different from him, when it came to trustworthiness. He wondered if he saw these co workers and the woman who betrayed his love as a constant reminder of his possible defense mechanism in relationships.

Once a female co worker made advances toward him while her husband waited in the parking lot outside of their workplace. Of course he didn't reject the advances, but it fed his beliefs of mistrust in a relationship, sustaining these beliefs even more in his life. It seemed as though everything in his environment added fuel to his mistrust. Where could he find anyone in his life to change his feelings and attitudes toward women in relationships.

Having had an interest in poetry, and attempting often to be a poet, he attended a poetry meetup group one afternoon. The experience did encourage his desire to write. While at the meetup a woman sat down next to him, it was the only available seat at the time. They had a relatively courteous conversation and decided to meet for lunch in the near future. Having talked on the phone several times, they then met for lunch. It turned out she had taught creative writing, and even at a university level. She saw much promise in his writing ability. His writing technique flowed when he started to put ideas in print, and it amazed her. It seemed he had an ability to put socially pertinent thoughts together easily, and at the same time hold one's interest. Seeing his writing on paper clarified what he felt and believed. He wrote events in his life, each to be dealt with individually, not as total way of life. He believed she wanted him to succeed and wanted the best for him. It turned out that was all she ever wanted for him. She had unlocked the prison within him that held all his fears about relationships, pardoning them and freeing him through writing.

They met frequently, during which time they pursued their wish of putting their poetry in book form, first together then individually. Politically their views were alike, and socially they enjoyed times out together. Her ideas of entertainment were new to him, but he learned to appreciate them. She saw him as rough around the edges, but very likable, as did her friends, and family. The same was true of her with the people in his life. Many from both sides noticed that they complimented each other, and made the other more complete. Though both were dominating personalities, they each had the desire and ability to stroke each other's heart with words and behavior.

Eventually he realize he had lost the need to protect his emotions. Everything about her was trustworthy in his mind. They did have issues at times, but it was never over fidelity or disrespect of each other. He began to like this new feeling within him. He didn't think she would do anything to hurt him. It seemed to him the more he trusted in her, the more his paranoia faded. Subsiding paranoia, and the growth of trust not only made him much more comfortable in the growing relationship, but seemed to encourage her kindness and concern had created a relationship for his well being. A chance meeting at a poetry group developed into a powerful, loving and trusting couple. His self defeating, happiness rejecting behavior had been put to rest, once he cut off the nourishing supply of his mistrusting defense mechanism and ignorance of self. A defense mechanism out of control and out of common sense; his behavior should have been the only thing he mistrusted.

In The Shadows

What I fear and see as downfalls, is only me
In shadows, my irrationalism waiting patiently
For me to do the counsel of nonsensical fears
Waiting - always waiting to walk me away in tears...

I alone walk me down a path of self destruction
Joining hateful speak and entitlements unearned,
I won't cry when I'm dismissed and left away sad
None can make me evil, it's done all on my own...

Evil is a leader only as long as I follow in its step
Enticed or beguiled I join evil by my own choice,
Temptation is only an offer of what won't ever be
Selfishly trading for evil, accept the consequences...

Terms of evil are always in the small print of life,
Details of what is, not should be, are neglected,
Fears are simply faith in evil, its threat of death
Can I say that death is truly my own beginning...

Let evil wait and wait until waiting is of no use
I leave it waiting as it waited the day I was born,
Don't let me be the one it walks away with in joy
Trust the love promised if we promise and love...

Tin Town

Tin Town was a section of the projects off of Seville Road in Cleveland, Ohio. It was called the New Projects, the area where we lived. The buildings were made of a corrugated metal, each building housed two families, and had a common crawl space above the ceiling. The other section of projects was called the old projects. If memory serves me well, there may have been two families in those buildings also. They were made of some type of chalk board covered with shingles, and they had coal bins outside for a heating supply; whereas the new projects had gas heating, with a space heater in the middle of the living room to heat the entire home.

Though it was part of Cleveland, it seemed as though it was a city unto itself. There was a precursor to a shopping mall. The word "mall" hadn't been heard of yet, at least not by the people living there in the early nineteen fifties. There was a grocery store named Fisher Foods, (that later became Abood's Foods), a beauty parlor, a dry cleaners, and a drug store all under one roof, but they all had separate entrances. Also existing there at the time was a small corner grocery store just known as "Oatman's", and another store of the same kind we called "Eli's". Both of those stores were a longer walk for those in Tin Town. The two smaller stores stayed open later than the larger grocery store, and that's when the smaller stores did most of their business, when the larger store closed.

There were two playgrounds, a smaller one for younger children, known as (The Little playground), and a larger playground (The Big

Playground) with a higher sliding board, and bigger swings. The center, as we called it, was actually a recreation center that had dances for teens on the weekends, checkers pool, and Bible School during the summer. There was a volleyball net and a horseshoe pit outside of the center. The maintenance building was connected to the center also. In the summer we illicitly obtained nails and boards for our different building projects including huts, scooters, and push carts from the maintenance building supply area.

Tin Town was a very special place. We knew the ins and outs, and ideosychrosies of just about every family living there, and when a new family moved in, it wasn't long before their children, and adults got to know ours as well. It can be said with a reasonable amount of accuracy, that it was probably the poorest of the poor in the Cleveland area.

There was a good mix of single parent homes and homes with two parents. It was a poor environment, and when I think back, every family there could have been categorized as poor. To me it seems the advantage of most everyone being poor was, that there was no one to look down on. We all seemed to mature at the same rate, develop and recognize special abilities and be known for them throughout the community.

Friendships of a lifetime began there, and memories of happiness sprouted there. The late nineteen fifties saw the demise of the projects in that area. The people living there were dispersed to different areas of Cleveland, where we were exposed to different classes of people, and saw how poor we really were. Some managed to excel in their new environments and many fell by the wayside. Death claimed its share, along with prisons, according to newspaper reports, but many survived and survived well. Though it seemed the ones that turned to crime were the more gentle fun loving individuals. The tough kids remained tough, and the personable people adjusted and or excelled in different areas of society.

Through all of stages of maturity I never saw happiness the way I experienced it in Tin Town. When I dream of happy places and friends I treasure, it's from there. Sadly I can never go back there, because "there" doesn't exist anymore. Tin Town was a place in time, a growing period, a place where self determination began. Simply put, it was home.

I've lived many other places, and at various levels of socio -economic existence, but when I reflect on happier times, it's always that place. It does perplex me how one can be so happy in poverty, and so restless the farther he is removed from that level. Maybe I should say Tin Town was a poor, but yet a rich environment, because there are other kinds of wealth not always recognized by society. No other time period of my life stands as tall in my memory, or as gentle in my heart.

Living At Home

Of all the places I've lived I still live at home
Houses occupied may only be dwellings -
What I call home may be a poor house
Your castle may live like a dump to me

Home is my heart, Tin Town is home
Happiness dwarfs the sad in that place
When I wish to be elsewhere, it's there -
The people and the place stay the same

I visit my home often, but can't go there
It doesn't exist, except living in my mind -
At a time it was there and I was there to
Learning what happy was and was not '

Poverty may bring ill thoughts to some
But it gives so much more than it takes -
Knowing what it is to be humble in life
And knowing humble's good in others

Vanity, vanity, oh vanity flee from me...

Roads To Eternity

Truths denied are lies empowered
We can say who we are -
But be who we say we aren't
Lies empowered by truths denied
We do what we say we don't -
But say we don't
Truths denied are lies empowered
We see what we live -
But not how we live
Lies empowered by truths denied
We speak what we say -
But not what we're saying
Truths denied are lies empowered
We hear what's true -
But it goes unheard
Lies empowered by truths denied
We know what to touch -
But it goes without feeling
Truths denied are lies empowered
We know what to love -
But it goes without an embrace...

A Friend Of Our Family

Good day everyone, my name is Reese, and I'd like to say what I know of Gordon who we've come to pay our respects to this day. I found out like I suppose some of you found out about his demise. We were waiting for the friend of our family to arrive for the holiday, when we heard the news on television. A commuter plane had crashed killing all six aboard. When they gave the name of the pilot and destination we knew all too well it was our friend of the family. Gordon had told me that he would catch a flight with a pilot friend of his to visit us.

Gordon was a friend that I had known from the time I was in college studying to be a nurse and he was a political science major. He had ambitions that went beyond any of mine or our other friends. He had always been extremely vocal in his support of equality among citizens of our society, especially the equal distribution of justice nationwide.

I had followed his career through infrequent contacts with him, but also through local and national news outlets. It was easy to keep up with his progress, because his political career had been so successful. It didn't hurt his career at all, that he was loved by voters in all factions. I could go on and on about such a positive life but won't. He was a modest person and I'd like to give others a chance to share what they know of him... And that was all Reese had to say concerning the friend of his family. Many more spoke, and surprisingly not all so glowingly, but respectfully; all seemed to be honest individuals.

Later that same day in a different part of town Paul is talking to a friend outside of a funeral home.

"Yeah Robert, it's really sad about Preston".

"What I can't figure out Paul, is, what was he doing on the same plane with all those important people".

"Ray, he was just someone from the neighborhood that chose to leave it. Besides, none of us kept in touch with him nor he us after he went into the military. I guess he made it pretty big there and was traveling with some congresswoman. Well Robert, let's get back inside it looks like they're getting ready to start Preston's funeral".

In still another part of Cleveland, Ohio, Roger is talking to Homer telling him about the death of their friend Lea. "I always thought she would die from an overdose. I never imagined her dying in a plane crash".

"Neither did I Roger, the last I heard she was dating some pilot that flew big shots up and down the east coast".

"I wonder how she ended up there Homer".

"Well Roger I heard she met this pilot at some event here in Cleveland, and he was really taken by her, to a good place in his life".

"She was a great person, Homer, I secretly had a crush on her, I really did. She just never got over her separation from Drake".

"Roger, she tried and tried, but kept going back to abusing drugs. I guess she felt no pain, when she was using, and maybe that's the only way she could make it. But I did hear last year, that she was getting her life together".

"You know Homer, I really don't think I'm going to the funeral. I'll pay my respects to her during the wake, but the funeral would just tear me to pieces. I keep picturing her and the rest of us as teens and young adults, too painful my friend".

"Roger I have to go to the funeral; man she was one of us! I think you should reconsider and go".

Okay I'll think about it.

Gordon, Preston, and Lea, three individuals from three different lifestyles ended up on a plane that was to take them together to eternity their eternity, their particular judgement.

Lea awoke from a sleep wondering where she was - Now standing in the presence of the Greatest Light. Without a word spoken, Lea knew that she was about to review her life, the good, and the evil, in comparison to the two commandments of The Son of the Most High. The great two commandments are: First - Thou shalt love the Lord thy God with all thy heart, and with all thy soul, and with all thy mind. Second - Love one another as I have loved you. Knowing these two great commandments innately, at this point. Lea lowered what she believed to be her head. As she lowered what seemed to be her head area, she felt a soul shaking disturbance within. Her head felt as though it was expanding and contracting violently. As the feeling subsided, out from her head came a being.

A being small in stature, displaying very sharp alien features and very large eyes, at least alien to anything Lea knew. Its colors varied and changed gradually and constantly. Then it spoke as it stood half bent and partially kneeling to her left front, facing The Greatest Light. "I am of legion. My family dwelled in her mind for more years than not that she lived, and she welcomed us. We own her?". Lea knew that she had in reality worshipped her drug use, for she had put her drug use before anything and anyone. She also knew that she had lacked humility, because she had been too proud to admit her sin due to unwarranted pride in a sinless life, she wished to appear to be living. Rather than diligently seeking help from Heaven or elsewhere she slothfully wallowed in her sin. Silently the Greatest light spoke without words, and Lea knew that these were her greatest sins, sins damaging her and the hearts of those that loved her.

The exit of the being of legion left her feeling totally clean, feeling and knowing faith in The Greatest Light, and with innocence existing at birth. But it was not the same Lea as she was at the moment of her death. Lea had the stains on her soul where the being of legion and its minions dwelt, and she wished it to be cleansed. What she presented to the greatest light was a brutalized soul.

Preston awoke from his sleep, wondering where he was, the same as Lea had done. He too found himself standing before The Greatest Light. He too knowing from The Greatest Light, the two great commandments. Then Preston's entire being shook violently, expanding, contracting, vibrating, and then several beings exited through different areas of his being all speaking at once, and all with numerous accusations. He wept uncontrollably, for then he knew that evil can never be good, and what's good can never be evil. He too knew faith in the Greatest Light, and his innocence at birth. The way all are before becoming a place of habitation for those of legion. "He is ours?", those beings identifying themselves as of legion said. They appeared to have no signs of weakness. Nor did they seem to be at a loss for a variety of accusations of Preston's character. Preston, now without the beings inhabiting him, was acutely aware of his sinning against God the Almighty, and against men, women and children in many countries of this earth.

Preston had admired the image of the soldier since childhood. After becoming a military man he had killed innocent individuals while they begged for mercy in the name of God. He committed terrible acts of cruelty under the guise of serving his country, and serving his country brought him praise at home. He was intoxicated by his authority over those weaker, he relished his superiority on the battlefield, and the admirations of his fellow citizens. He flaunted his uniform and what it represented. What it represented to most, was not what it represented to him.

He realized now, that being a soldier had only been a symbol of power for ruthlessness, and admiration. Now he found himself surrounded by those of legion accusing and attempting to claim him. He knew his soul had been greatly damaged beyond repair, for he had never reconciled his sins in truth and deeds, prior to his moment of death, and had allowed those of legion that dwelt there for such a long period, free to invite others of them, to dwell there also.

Gordon woke from his sleep, and immediately knew where he was. He had worshipped enemies of Heaven knowingly, for worldly gain. The beings of legion exited his existence from every possible direction. The beings gone, Gordon said without a spoken word to The Greatest Light, that he had chosen another to worship rather than God The Almighty. He had known that his greed, vanity, lust, and envy of anyone who possibly had more than he, material wise, was evil. In his truthfulness he admitted to valuing worldly gains over a Heavenly eternity, and denied the authority of The Son of Man in spoken word, though he knew the truth. The beings jumped and shouted all types of accusation, never repeating one. Those of legion gleefully proclaimed in unison, "We know he is ours?". Gordon recognized his shredded soul. He groaned and cried out in his despair.

The Greatest Light informed each of the three, without spoken word, to observe the three paths behind them. The three individually observed the three paths. What each of them saw when they looked down the first path was a bright place filled with joyous song, pleasing fragrances, and beautiful rivers with lovely sounds of the water. Occasionally they all observed an individual making their way on the first path, dragging what seemed to be a broken chain behind them. The second path viewed showed a darkened place with high constant flames, and souls prostrating themselves. Their voices were in constant prayer, praising Heaven, and crying out "mercy dear Lord mercy; dear Lord have mercy on we". Down the third path they saw giant flames, and screams expressing "Damned forever we be, damned forever, for our suffering has no end".

Finally words came from The Greatest Light instructing them to "Take your place in eternity". Lea immediately tried heading for the first path, but found herself being pulled to the second or third path. Lea attempted to force her will on what held her back from making it to the first path. She looked down and saw the being of legion trying to take her to the third path. Lea resisted harder, as did her accuser. Finally the resistance ceased and she found herself entering the second path, and as she entered the flames, the being of legion was consumed by the flames. Lea prostrated herself and began to praise Heaven and beg for mercy from our Lord and God The Almighty.

Preston the soldier was a vanquished soul, and was experiencing the ruthlessness of those many of legion that overpowered his desire for the first or second path, their field of battle superiority of numbers appearing around him. As they dragged him down the third path he howled "No, No, I'm sorry, I'm sorry". He and the beings entered the flames, but those of legion were consumed by the flames as they were destined to run towards and into them.

Gordon was immediately seen being pulled to the third path, and screaming "Fool, foolish me, just a fool, only a fool seeks and works to earn a place in damnation. Death, death, forever death we live", and those of legion were taken by the flames.

All I Can Handle

Before judging others by my morals
I should believe mine are of salvation
Lesser deem a lesser eternity
Achieving salvation is all I can handle
To each their own be it life or death
Let the dead bury the dead, not me -
I'll not judge by the world no not at all

Judging me is all I can Handle in life
I can seek others like me sharing joy
In what the world has not, nor ever can -
The world shall take if I allow it, my faith,
In doing so my hope of my eternal life
Before judging others by my morals
I should be sure mine are of salvation

Down The Road

In my mature years I tend to believe life has been a series of poems and situations. Poems often remembered as songs of happiness, sadness, bitterness, and fear. Situations lived and remembered as hopes, dreams, failures, rebuilding, and evaluating. It seems as though all poems and situations have combined in ways to bring me to the point where I choose to believe that I could not have had a better preparation for where I should and need to go from here, which probably could have been said at any point in my life.

If I had had the wisdom to recognize poems and situations for what they truly were, ways to go or avoid, ways of love or leaving, ways to purchase or sell, and ways to believe or reject life's encounters Then I may have had more pleasurable poems and less stressful situations to live.

Nothing we do in life is absorbed into a void. We leave trails of pain, anxiety, tears, regret, as well as smiles, anticipation, love and happiness. Our choices in life determine which we leave the most of behind. All choices have to be reconciled at some point, but at which point do we choose reconciliation. Hopefully choosing sooner, rather than a neglected reconciliation.

Good I have

Good I have is my learning and believing
In what was, is, and shall forever be true -
Being Christian invites cruelty for now
A world trying to dash all of Christ's truths
Truths can't be changed - only lied about

Mocking, discrimination, and real violence
Is what this world brings to all Christians -
Hoping to draw them to an eternal death
Setting one on a road to certain perdition
The watchers chose, and now directing us...

Good I have is my learning and believing
That this world only offers and delivers
Temptation of the body to ruin a sad soul -
Weakened souls in sadness may succumb
Sadness from envy, greed, anger or more...

Good I have is my learning and believing
Christ's teachings imitated and obtained
Delivers all from the worldly weaknesses -
A price of a burden, "it be" good to pay
To choose Christ over anything in this world...

In Prayer

Show me Mother the offers in the annunciation -
In choosing in agony to suffer now for Father
Leading to our own resurrection's glorious day
Announce - Choose - and Receive

Show me Mother to visit every visit in Christ
Experiencing worldly scourging along the way
A reward of ascension to His prepared place
Visit in Christ - Suffer in Christ - Rise to Christ

Show me Mother to know the Teacher from birth
Rejecting all crownings meant to mock His good
A Good descending to comfort us until a return
Know birth - Know mocking - Know Holy Ghost

Show me Mother His pleasing presentation
With diligence and strength of carry of the cross
Recognizing an assumption to a Heavenly place
Be presentable - imitate the carry - trust assumption

Show me Mother to be found in my temple as He
Let my faith be as His even if facing a crucifixion
I ask for prayers, Heavenly Mother Crowned Queen
Work in faith - Die in faith - know our Mother's love

Chibobbit

Unbeknownst to the catholic priest that had performed the rite, Chibbobit was recently exorcised in Northern Ireland from a person who was native of England. It'd been driven from a guilty person in an unsolved murder. The person moved from London, and settled in the United States. The individual went on to in status, a model citizen; his ethics never challenged in society. He rose to a position many would envy. Though he never visited a catholic place of worship ever again, he was seen as an outstanding member of society. Chibobbit had inhabited the individual so well, that it chose to mirror his settlement in the United States. The demon found no entrance into the being he had once called his possession. That was the individual from which it was driven out. Chibobbit was now searching for a new temple to inhabit. Though a well practiced demon, it seemed to prefer the possession of the innocent.

The demon entered a home on Craven avenue in Cleveland, Ohio. Though the house was occupied by many individuals, only one, an infant, not yet a toddler, looked the demon in the eye, and began to say "Chibobbit, Chibobbit,". A couple of the adults asked what the child had said. Another adult just claimed it was baby talk. Chibobbit decided to become this child's invisible friend. It entertained the child with such antics, that it caused cries of laughter from the child. It became a constant companion, stimulating the child to all types of overt responses, that caused some of the family to take notice, but not interest, since after all he wasn't crying. He was laughing, just staring or frowning, at many action, but never crying. He's a good boy, they thought to themselves, and said openly in conversation. They often looked at the child and just smiled at his so called good behavior.

As the child grew his words of Chibobbit became songs of the invisible friend, "Chibobbit Chibobit, Chibobit fly, Chibobbit try to go in or out of my eye. Chibobbit sing Chibobbit bring friends to play ring. Chibobbit not hot Chibobbit not cold, he say I be bold".

The child eventually became aggressive with other children, and challenged adult authority. His parents chalked it up to him just exerting his independence, which they believed to be a good development. They both suggested that an invisible friend was quite normal in some children's growth. As the child grew he dedicated more and more of his time to his invisible friend. The parents expressed their recognition of his isolated behavior, but failed to address it. They believed the child to be developing somewhat faster intellectually, than most of the children in his surroundings.

When the child started school, his parents could not have been more pleased with his academic development. His physical abilities surpassed any of the other children, but it seemed he just preferred to play alone. Though he played alone, the child never seemed to be alone. At school or at home he seemed to have the most fun while playing alone. He would go off into the woods for hours and then return home, seemingly wiser than when he woke that morning.

By the time he was in his early teens, he was rather dismissive of his parents and their authority. He was able to out reason any attempt they made to control him. The mother was concerned, but the father was proud, saying he expected the child to go a long way in this world. The father also proposed that someday everyone in the country would know his son's name. He became more supportive of his son's undesirable behaviors and dismissive of the mother's concerns. The son heard his father tell his mother, "Don't you recognize a genius when it is there before your very eyes ?". The mother replied "Why did you use the term "it", when speaking of our child ? He heard his father reply, "I don't know, the word "it", just came out when I spoke". The child looked through the crack in the door and saw a very perplexed expression on his father's face. The child turned to his friend and asked it, what do you think of all this ? Chibobbit said he believed they needed to rid themselves of them both, but nothing could be done until they were able to leave home and live on their own, their way.

"Grigori is your name", Chibbobit said. "Are you changing my name to Gregory" The child asked? "No" Chibobbit replied with a hint of indignation and irritation, "it's Grigori just as I said, G-r-i-g-o-r-i. Remember that as long as I choose to be your friend. Otherwise Grigori, our friendship will come to an abrupt and permanent end. Then who will you have to develop you in my image".

"I've taught you more than any school could ever teach you and I've given you, in my ways, the strength to out do any of your type physically. Whatever you are Grigori, I made and gave to you". The teen then said, "Everything but a girlfriend. Since you call me Gregory I'll name you Chibby, since you look as though you should be much taller?". Chibbobit then told the child that he is taller than the child could ever imagine. Chibbobit then said to him "The name is Grigori human, Grigori" he yelled angrily, "and yes you may call me by that name". "Okay Chibby how about the girlfriend" the child asked. He replied, "in time human, in time. I'll call you Grig". "Sure" the child replied, "makes no nevermind to me", he added sarcastically. He merely frowned and then smiled a little at the child's insolent attitude.

Chibobbit told the child that he should talk his parents into sending him to a special school for children like him He believed that Grig would find out there, just where he fit into a world that held no interest worth his attention. Sure enough, when the child told his parents about this school for what some would call exceptional children, his father was immediately on board to send him there, but his mother looked a little perplexed, because she felt the only thing special about her child was his arrogance and selfishness. She did finally go along with her husband and the idea of sending the child to the special school.

The research the mother did on the school showed that a vast number of accomplished individuals had graduated. Many of those individuals had reviewed and endorsed the school, and all the children had found the school on their own and then brought the school to the attention of their parents. When the child and his parents visited the school they noticed most of the young men were of the same temperament as their child, and the young women were no different, superior attitude, and athletically outstanding. The mother also felt the name of the school was unusual; it was called "Mount Hermon, School for Exceptional Children" and the logo was "Legion" planted boldly over a herd of some type of beings. The name of the school concerned her to the point of bringing the matter to the attention of her Priest. A friend advised her to read the Book of Enoch, and told her, if she had any further questions to contact her priest. Her concerns were elevated after reading the Book of Enoch, and she addressed them to her husband, who immediately dismissed them as well. When she addressed the child as to how he came to learn of the school, he disrespectfully said, "It's no nevermind of yours, bye". Then turned and walked away.

She went home in tears due to the lack of support from her mate and the total disrespect shown her by her offspring. She sought the counsel of her priest, who enlightened her on known possessions of humans by demons. So much about her child pointed to his possible possession by the unholy. She found herself walking in the wooded area behind their home, and finding peace in prayer, because it seemed prayer brought understanding and clarity to her situation.

One day while walking in the wooded area, she came upon a small hut. In the hut were roots, berries, and foul smelling liquids in small bottles labeled "potion", each with a different number. Along with those items she found a journal in her child's handwriting which referenced Chibobbit and its teachings. These findings confirmed her beliefs of her child's possession. She went back to her house and got her small bottle of holy water that she kept for blessing certain items in the home. She returned to the hut, and sprinkled holy water throughout the tiny structure and then set it ablaze. As she turned to leave, she saw her child standing in her path. He began to change colors, slowly but constantly.

He snorted, moaned, and then killed her with a blow to the side of her head with a solid walking stick.

He dragged her body into the wooded area, and she was never heard from again. He told his father she had left with a man as he was returning home, and they were holding hands. The father mourned, but seemed to find solace in the fact that he still had his child, whom he felt was even more precious after his wife left him for another man. He started indulging the child's every demand, because the child no longer simply ask for anything. Everything he desired became demands.

The father of the child was even more pleased when he learned his child, now a young man, had obtained a degree in ministry and planned to build his very own church. His church would be built with the counsel of Chibby. Grig's faith in Chibby was far stronger than his faith in anyone or anything else. He and Grig agreed that all members of his church must share the same beliefs as Chibby. Though the congregation would never meet Chibby, they would certainly know him through Grig.

Grig became adept at manipulating, misrepresenting and cherry picking chapters and verses from the Holy Scriptures to make his agenda palatable and even more pleasing to church members, these were the intentions Chibby had for the visions and directions of Grig's church. The vision for the church was that it be the last and final interpretation of the holy scriptures; according to Grig, according to Chibby! Through Grig, Chibby's influence would grow into a religion meant to satisfy Chibby's taste for young souls, and if the parents had to be cultivated in order to develop the source of feeding, all the better. Chibby believed Grig could cultivate the parents and Chibby would own the souls of the innocent. Because Chibby had influenced the child's father through Grig and that turned out to be very satisfying to Chibby. Though Grig had murdered his mother because she couldn't be cultivated and was on a path to dealing with her son's possession when she took her concerns to her priest. Her priest when made aware of her concerns, doubted the manufactured story of her leaving. Though he couldn't disprove

Grig's account of her leaving, he did pray for truth and resolution of the matter.

Grigori's church flourished. The parents of the children of Mount Hermon School for Exceptional Children all became members, bringing the already prepped children with them. Outstanding in their communities were these children and parents, successful people in some areas of society. They were admired by members of the modest communities which they chose to inhabit. New ideas of how present laws bound them to a stagnant existence, and the only way out was to go against those laws. They endorsed the ideas that drugs were okay and violence was an act of resistance. They fostered igniting the belief that drug dealing was a way out of a stagnant life, because after all, the people bringing the drugs to the country were gaining great wealth, and if it took violence to survive in that life, let it be that way.

Those who succumbed to the influence of the church, joined the church and brought the children along. Through the haze of violence, drugs and money, the communities never saw the hell existing around them. Chibby was pleased as were all those from Mount Hermon. The women took pride in the most eccentric forms of makeup and dress, they delved into spells, signs, and counterspells. The men obtained more powerful means of intimidation through greater weaponry. Chibobbit's influence through Grigori was flourishing. They had begun to contemplate drinking the blood of their innocent, and maybe, just maybe, someday sacrificing an infant for the members of the church to consume. Saying it would allow them to possess the purest souls and direct them in any direction Grig thought appropriate. Chibobbit occasionally suggested the idea to the child in a playful, or not so playful way. Grig saying "Yeah I might like that". It pleased Chibby to see how casually Grig accepted the thought.

Chibobbit "like" beings were to gain entry into the souls of the parents and their young. Those who were already on the road to being owned by "Chibby likes". What thrilled Chibby was the thought of countless young souls being taken as he had taken Grig when not yet toddler, an imaginary friend that was anything but imaginary. Grig had one parent that was suspicious of the behavior of the child, but she met her demise and the other was pleased by the behavior, and that left no resistance to those calling the child's soul home.

The church had developed a council, whose task it was to lay out the future of the church for the next three and a half years and beyond. The plans sought to bring them closer to their god, the god of Chibobbit, by infecting the congregation and inhabiting the newborns who were unfortunate enough to be born within. Then they would expand the church by developing more children like Grig. When Grig informed Chibby of the plan, Chibobbit feigned a surprise response, as Chibby already knew. Grig still had not recognized Chibby's realm of knowing. Though Chibby shared much with Grig, he didn't share all about himself.

The church's leaders and the most dedicated members gathered one evening to review their goals and paths to their goals. Praises were heaped upon Grig for the way he had brought the church to a position of prominence and influence. Grig had the attention of many women in his congregation, as was promised earlier in their relationship between him and Chibby. The celebration turned into an all out orgy of indulgence by all present. Guns were presented for sale in the community, for a show of strength, according to Grig through Chibby. Drugs stocks were examined and some used for the celebration, because after all, most of the drugs were needed to control of their community, and the surrounding ones. Near the end of the celebration Grig brought forth a small marble table mounted on a wooden stand. The marble was sunken in the middle that measured about the size of a baby's bath tub. Grig proclaimed it as their soul garden.

With that proclamation the skies darkened, the clouds churned and an EF-5 tornado ended all plans and hopes of the, (now screaming for God's mercy), church congregation. A two by four piece of wood picked up by the tornado was carried a distance and struck a man, removing his head. It was the man "It" (Chibby) had been driven out of in Northern Ireland. The man had finally received his just dues, "It" (Chibby) thought as he and the inhabitants of the souls of the congregation were taken into nothingness, never again to inhabit a child of God, where

they wait for the final Judgement. The congregation went to their
particular judgement.

Please Don't Feed The Animals

Upon entering a blue zoo, the keeper says -
Please don't feed the animals
Their diet is to maintain stability in the zoo
A zoo requires animals to be controlled
A threat and a reward system of living here
Is what makes living here in sync possible

In sync with the zoo is preferable to self
Please don't feed the animals
A zoo diet determines one's zoo life
Animals must believe what we feed is so
So is preferable to natural leading along
Leading along is following ways of the zoo

The zoo is observed from up and down
Watchers feed and stars wait anxiously
Some animals eat and some fast faithfully
Both knowing but not when freedom is due
Bringer of justice for the world and of each
A final Server not reversible or for a penitence

A paradise for man became an animal zoo
Some perform for the zoo yet others don't
A choice in the zoo leads to a life outside
A chosen life of death or a life of life to be
The zoo is cages and all offered the same
Fasting and starving in the zoo is life soon
Thriving in a zoo is a certain path to death

Mysterious

Promised good times are coming
So let me feel the coming's joy
The visit in joy and humbleness
Let me visit all my days as such
Justice is born no one is exempt
I want to live in just and rightness
A presentation approved on High
Praying my presentation is like
Found working as heritage is
Find me in my temple doing right

Agony felt for what must be done
I'll choose with strength granted
Pain endured for the will of One
I may persevere with granted Will
Mocked and maligned for truth
I shall not fall to indignations fed
Carried truth to death is honor
My truth is my burden in this life
Dying gave life for all times now
Let my death be my life to come

Leaving death in the wake of life
Burying death is my goal after it
Gone to welcome or condemn
Being welcomed home is heritage
The Knowing Truth left behind
I've learned to listen when spoken
Taken up to advocate for children
I know Mother's love is perfect
Crowned as my Queen for all time
My love and respect belongs to Her

See Me See You

Know not me nor my name,
Tell me what you think you see
What you see isn't me but you,
Be it good or bad it's your truth...

Love felt for me is love in you,
A goodness making you smile
And sending beams of kindness
Kindness we feel as we pass...

Dismissiveness sent my way,
You see such as consuming
But you know it consumes you,
Projecting it on me as we pass...

Pain, which is seen as we pass
Wrenching and grinding there,
Squeezing and eroding sent to me
Reflecting you truly as we pass

Oppression seen in me by you
Tell me what smites you daily,
Finding fellowship in suffering ?
A fellowship now as we pass

Trust viewed in me as we pass
Do you see me as you see you ?
Should I not be seen as you see
Is there trust by you as we pass ?

Hate for me is clear as we pass
Vaporized and released into air
Breathed back in by you to live
To dwell comfortably as we pass

Sadness observed while passing
My sadness is truly your sadness
Radiated from within your heart
Sadly engulfing you as we pass

Peace in a heart gives and takes
Giving a need and taking a same
Peace overcomes emotions sting
Touching each soul as we pass

Compassion shared as we pass
A heartfelt focusing known by us
A relief experienced in real chaos
Confusion lost for now as we pass

Learn to know me and I know you
Growth is seen by what's learned
Pleasure exist in all to be shared
Share each others' as we pass

Say goodbye mutually as we pass
So much learned, lost, and saved
In and out of our cages of our truth
Observing in a zoo as we pass

The blue zoo makes me feel a little silly, a little angry, and sometimes
sane. I tend to keep in mind that it's only a zoo, and meant to observe

behavior and measure an outcome from directions. Outcomes measured are outcomes totally under the control of the individual being measured by opposite sides. One side cheers for better outcomes in an individual's measurements, while the other encourages or entices toward outcomes foreign to the individual's innate measurements. In effect, this makes a different individual, from the one initially intelligently designed, and not one hatefully mutated. Accepting or rejecting the reality of a zoo life does matter. Every exhibit is being observed by the other exhibits in the zoo. Either way it may cause one to be a little silly, a little angry, and sometimes sane.

The exhibits

I The Squirrel

A child displaying pure energy
Surefooted as a mountain goat
Able to dazzle often with speed
Daring to an almost grave level
Cute but didn't realize that truth
In love with what he believes true
Living in innocence is truly bliss

Me The Coyote

A preteen made by surroundings
Not sure just where I truly belong
Walking easily as to not misstep
Periods of an influenced courage
Wanting to blend and to lead me
Truly unaware of correct direction
Living in chaos is no place to stay

I The Lynx

Strong and lonely with confidence
Just seeking to develop all alone
Yet constantly measuring myself
Fearing greater yet passing such
Never competing with any lesser
Unable to share such a lonely life
Lonesome living in a partial world

Me the Alley Cat

A young arrogant sort owning all
Owning and boasting of nothing real
Outburst undue and ill conceived
Wanting all my kin to walk softly
Sowing wild oats foolishly done
So terrifying alone or with my kin
Arrogance absent wisdom is foolish

I The Wolf

Overseeing the pack's well being
Gentleness and power I now own
Protecting what will give me a me
In growing the pack's dominance
I'll command and protect for now
Until the day I succumb to fatigue
Fatigue that will will end my rule

Me the Bear

Older, more confident and wiser
I see my tracks and path ahead
Knowing my rights from my lefts
And the ups and downs are so clear
I teach in silence and with motion
Now seeing around and too within
A pinnacle reached by my growth

I the Aged Buck

On the edge of my predator's list
Stiff and losing speed and agility
Waiting in a line of those before me
I keep getting closer to the front
My time will come to feed the flow
And rest on the plains of this world
A monument bleached by the sun

Drawers

A nursing student working for the summer
Working as an orderly in the sixties
Called for duties all over the hospital
Observing things he hoped to be doing
Doing someday as a Registered Nurse

A call for him from a unit one afternoon
(Presented the beginning of a picture) -
One which would haunt him for his career
One day he took a dead body to a morgue
Cold and quiet, an unmistakable smell

The cold door the cold tray sliding out
Thinking how unavoidable it is for all

No matter how or where we die -
The morgue is one of our final stops
A thought of his career impression
Respect dearly the dead we meet
I'll silently meet the orderly transporting
Me to that silent stopover on my way out

More To Me

Do you realize our time together
May mean more to me than you
All of you living in my memories
Moments, hours, days, or years
I tend to treasure and relive each

Sad moments I throw to the side
Pleasures and love in memories
Are my entertainment to watch
I can smile and love in the movie

Shows that belong to me for life
Some shared, and others to keep
Kept in a vault that's in my mind
And released to me on demand

A demand that is placed by me
Reliving what we lived back then
When our time together was two
Now the two may only be my one

All things are as they were then
Like we were my movie, I a star
Many in my life came and went
As though they were just extras
Playing their parts in what I live

Leaving any sadness lived then
On my minds cutting room floor
I do ask because I really should
Do you realize our time together
May mean more to me than you

The Audition

I auditioned for a place in your life
But it seems I just did not fit into it
I wasn't the character you wanted
Yet I wanted you to want me then
But now the issue has been closed
I've been cut from your life forever
Knowing and yet not knowing why

I watched you move on and away
Until you were gone from my sight
Sometimes I see you telling me
That I don't belong in your life as me
So it seems all I can do now is go
And live as if I threw you to the side
Calling you a sadness is all I can do

Now lying on your cutting room floor
It seems you chose not to think of me
Now I must do the same in my mind
You're to my side, I'm out your door

What was the use of the time we had
Except to know we could not be one
Time well spent, and time not wasted

Trying

Business As Usual

I can show most who I really wish to be -
Eight hours a day, seven days a week.
I'm who you think I should be in every way.
You think you know who I am, and so do I.
You know the co worker, and a parishioner.
The co worker that's honorable and caring,
A parishioner that's God fearing and good.
Sixteen hours a day and seven days a week
I live that co worker when I'm not working -
A discriminating hateful drunk is in his shoes.
Without parishioners and co workers in place -
Within his mind, body, and soul are evil ways.
His ways during most of the hours of the day -
At work he's performing and also in Church.
Away it's merely business as usual for him
Discrimination, hatred, vanity, and greed
But the me I don't know I don't see -The true me

Gambling

Infidelity while in love is high stakes
Drinking and driving is a loser's bet
Cheating is betting you'll go around
Drug abuse is merely a losing hand
Hatred is overplaying a weak hand

Greed is playing the game too long
Vanity shows everyone your hand
Insensitivity is not seeing the cards

Living isn't playing life as a gambler
Nor is it trying not to choose at all
It's letting life happen not making it
Life is a series of choices we make
That may or may not unknowingly
Turn into a game of chance
Instead of peaceful lanes

Blame

Being influential is not what I thought it to be
One influenced and influencing is a chain link
Giving and taking what surrounds me is a life
A life blaming others for what I have chosen
To hold together what is in reality falling apart
Choices of losing truth and replacing it with lies
That I claim as mine but are teachings of others
No independence of thought - all reason gone

Time came when independence needed repair
Recognizing the losses I have lived and spread
Regret and shame overflowed my memories in life
Wondering how I could ever undo what I've done

Influences revisited that hindered good choices
In thought I had allowed the choices of others
To be my choices for the sake of wanting to belong
Wanting to belong to what and why such desires ?
An outsider wanting in to serve a chains purpose ?
Why the chain and what does it imprison in life ?

In independence I can suspect a wish to influence
Joining choices that seem to join mine and why
Having a measure of conscience all along the way
Choices of compassion and truth will serve me well

Blue

I do it each day with reluctance -
Out of necessity for an existence
My home holds my happiness in
Outside fosters chaos on the wind

Outside I run to my left and right
To avoid being taken over by tides
Tides of ill reason and of ill intent
In my home I move about unseen

Stores are a big part of my survival
Providing what I can't make myself
Avalanches of assault on my wages
Wages meant to reinforce my home

Christianity anchors what I believe
Outside floods of variances linger
Trying to cut my anchor so I drift
Away from what I believe is home

I move about in society where I exist
Because there's no other choice now
Where the snow drifts the blows dislike
For what God chose to make me now

Balance interrupted around my home
Earthquakes of sadness shake me

For the suffering of the less fortunate
Who cry on the run, later to lament
Making home a place for mourning

Hinges

Doors, gates and lids allow access
Entities may come, go or even stay
Stay and bring happiness to home
Leave having made good memories
One staying may have a big impact
On future happenings in this, my life

Gates may allow entrance to a yard
But not definite entry into a home
Leaving one outside of the of home
Until a reasoned evaluation is made
Open doors can reject or emit entry
Depending on what is brought

Once inside a home the lid is lifted
Off the true desire one brings in
Revealing what will be released
Inside the home or of the dwelling -
Place of an individual's living soul
Being construction or destruction

The strength of the home or soul
Defines the visitor's or intruder's
Ability to leave either one sound
Or to remain completing the leveling
And then move onto another one
Again to build or destroy upon entry

Many are they who wish to enter
Our place where goodness exist
To lay claim and inhabit territory
Where a soul may well be claimed

Teeth And Tears

I grit my teeth and shed my tears as I wake, walk or sleep. Shame on me for not knowing until now what is truly afoot. Self aware and self absorbed until self can't be penetrated. I saw with blinded eyes and felt with a numbness of touch, what existed outside of myself as I walked, woke or slept. I knew so much while not knowing at all what held me in. I was held in check by forces invasive to all inhabitants of earth. I was invaded by those forces because I allowed the invasion, as I walked, woke and slept calmly through the chaos about. Chaos designed to appear as man's order and fairness, but really only order and fairness for the privileged and powerful only. Leaving those of lesser means to be stroked while spat on !

When should I bare my teeth and show my tears in times of dismissiveness of justice and compassion by those of wealth and power to the meek and the forgotten? Baring my teeth at those who feign compassion and justice only to continue to enjoy benefits from the ills put on others? Shed my tears when I see the poor and the meek wander to places in their minds filled with illusions and delusions of a life promised with no intention of being fulfilled by those making the promises? I can bare my teeth at a world that made their world a truth?

Shedding my tears and hoping against hope each day of my life in a world that gives no hope of value in the Holy promise of justice? My hope is to be worthy to share the greater Holy promised, by sharing, and being compassionate and loving all as He loved?

My truth, friendship, love and peace in a world feigning such is to
bare my teeth and shed my tears always in defiance of those who would
make anyone lesser than they in life. Defending them with teeth bared
and consoling while tears
Shed

Bear With Me

Bear with me as I have with you as you defined
Truth
A truth that encouraged me to be less than you
Your truth
Truths created by man are not truths in anyway
Only God's truth is
God's word manipulated is no longer His truth
It's yours
Bear with me as I have with you as you defined
Friend
A friend to gain acceptance then misuse and hate
Your friendship
Friends that love and care at all levels of life
God's friendship
A friendship of disgrace, discard and evil ridicule
Has been your friendship
Bear with me as I have with you as you defined
Love
A love of self and the like and despisement of others
Your at knows no boundaries of compassion
God's love
A love of entitlement, power and nullification
Has been your love
Bear with me as I have with you as you defined
Peace
A peace around you while others are trodden on

Your peace
Peace in knowing that here is to decide the hereafter
God's peace
A peace in your home while mayhem is exported
Has been your peace

Ways of the world

Living A Lie

Hidden dependencies - Living life around a dependency -
And rarely revealing the individual gripped by an addiction.
Many moments of an interaction become an act on a stage -
With that person in the starring role and supporting actor too.
Lines are rehearsed and stage presence acutely developed -
And the closing of each show is followed by a sigh of relief.
A review of the performance is printed in the mind's column -
With suggested improvements to elevate the truthfulness.

Lose the dependency - and depend on real choices in life -
No rehearsals or scripts needed for the real truth is recorded.
Lines flow, mannerisms are original as are the lines presented -
Recorded as facts in the daily life of an individual living truly.

Public drunkenness - Flourishing in a public display of greed -
And rarely revealing what's been sacrificed for stately places.
Admired by some, questioned by others, but lost in excesses
Ones seeing themselves as models of success in every way
Models of what one becomes when one becomes so worldly
Ways of the world are their ways, Heavenly worship a show
Greed to be fostered and their compassion is for their own kind
The poor with them are for selfish use and then disposed of

Stop drinking from the cup of excess - and see the poor here
Compassion shall be unleashed to suffer and share with the poor
Refuse the next drink and avoid the curse of greed and vanity
What's done for the poor and meek is done in Heaven's name

Indecent exposure - When we rebuke love for the road of hate
Unwrapped and undressed, for all to see hate for hate's sake
Hoping to influence or engage others on that same road taken
Sometimes taken in the name of Heaven, other times in hell's
Cloaked in darkness, eloquence or fear smell the same
Around the corner or the block it can be heard if we wished to hear
In the forest or in the office it can be seen if we chose to see it
In the meat or in the water it can taste bitter should we consume

Lose the hatred - and lose those demons living in your temple
Make room for Heaven's goodness offered for Its acceptance
Put at bay and arrest the malignancy of illness of the unholy
Speak in peace, work life in peace, and live in Heavenly peace

Grand theft - When a life is taken in hate, calling it justifiable
Is a desired lie to excuse an inexcusable act of discrimination
The taker knows, the excuser knows, and Heaven knows too
Acts painted in a false suit of protection and in service
Honored by themselves and their cult in public and in private
Privately truth is told and known in jest and mock, all know it
An impenetrable force among us, given its authority over us
Authority to service and protect or to abuse and neglect any

End a service - to the unholy whom you are aware you serve
In too deep, pressure from peers, enjoying new found power
What is worldly given shall be taken or removed in this world
Face Judgement with confession, penitence and repentance

Government fraud- When one serves self and not the people
It is fraud of the most grievous kind, when a lie denies it
Saying wait and see, give it time and it'll be proven true
The liar will have feathered his bed and those of his contributors
While leaving the people to pay for philosophy's greed
Hoping to be retired or his promises forgotten, the liar hovers
In silence and feigned surprise the liar proposes a solution
A solution built on another fraud to reduce voters resolve

Handcuff lawmakers - Not allowing them to profit from laws
That they write and pass that voters don't receive the same
Healthcare should be no better than those that elected them
Retirement 'Entitlements" shall be prorated on a (20yr basis)

Bedtime

Time for bed you sleepy head
You've toiled and you've spoken
What's in your heart after a start
Living thoughts as were taught
Washed in light-night was a fight
Eyes closed in a peaceful repose
A curtain drawn ready for dawn
Rise and shine to your pathline
Live and praise for He the raised

High Society

Blue Zoo Prisons

By a donald

The brown stranger's interviews of the recently paroled and those that had completed their prison sentences seemed to have a common thread. A thread connecting what a person was before incarceration and the individual released on society after a portion or an entire sentence had been completed. Assault in different forms defined their survival during a sentence. Assaults were expressed in the form of rape, intimidation and bloodletting. Sometimes the person remained a victim and other times he became the one committing the assaults. Often, no matter the sexual orientation of the newly incarcerated, regardless of the lesser levels of aggression or the desire to become a successful product of prison rehabilitation, the individual was returned to society more damaged than he was before entering the prison system.

Because I don't see my failure - does it mean I didn't ?
If I don't feel your pain - does it mean you don't hurt ?
If my brother does die - does it mean dying means nothing ?
When I don't bleed - does it mean you're not losing blood?

I send you away in the name of rehabilitation - so I think
How you returned is more frightening - than you were before
Bringing what was on the inside - to the those down the street
Should I have sent you away - or to a place that I'd know ?

I sent you to hell - believing an angel would come home
You had to live - where most would perish on admission
So strong is survival in there - what was you strength before
I may never know - for your demons are controlling you now

I didn't care before you went in - but now I do that you're out
Never looked twice at you - because you were out of sight
Now I must look suspiciously at you - I know what I made
You stumbled hard and went - Where you went was my doing !

The hierarchy in prisons are the inmates who have found positions
of power and influence in a place we designed for rehabilitation of those
who need reminding of how society should flow. They've changed a
place that we created to restore civilized behavior into a place where they
tried to live in society before being sentenced. Ever changing and ever
so sporadic tyrants, depending on who may be the most violent at any
given moment, rule little kingdoms of oppression, collecting taxes, and
favors, brutality over those weaker or those wishing to be rehabilitated.

The weak live under their rule, or are not be allowed to live at all.
The oppressors have no fear of incarceration, because it's only going
home to them. It seems that incarceration is more comfortable for them
than following the processes of a civilized community. The processes of
prison are the ones of the mighty at the moment.

It seems that you've engaged society - and found it intolerable
Finding your way back to prison - you found your kind of society
Three hots and a cot - is your palace throne and throne room
Bars are your palace - and prison guards your palace guards

Prison cooks are your palace chefs - the weak your extra portions
Holding court in the prison yard - minions carry out your wishes
Contraband is your enterprise - protection is your sideline
Keeping peace among kingdoms - is the talk of the prison kings

War is avoided among the kingdoms - but fought in prison daily
The weak suffer from war fatigue - or find suicide or madness
The weak and the meek gone forever - left is only pieces of shadows
While the kings get fatter - awaiting more subjects to enter

Kings thrive and rule in prison - but couldn't as subjects on the outside
Brutalizers took rehabilitation - made it a factory of unsavory production
So successful they were - that their product was sold to a civilized society
Sodomy, rape and forced homosexuality now talk of comedy and acceptance

The donald returned to the Governor's office with his findings from interviewing vast numbers of parolees and those having finished their sentences. What he reported to the governor was in short, a need for a prison within prisons in the state. His findings suggested that the need for separating individuals who were preventing the rehabilitation of those on track for rehab or those truly desiring to be rehabilitated. Rapist in the prison population should be separated from the rest of the inmate population. Each time an inmate is raped, a violent crime has been committed against an individual in the state's care, and technically the state is derelict in its duty (since the person is in the care of the state) leaving the state open for punitive damages. The same could be construed as true in the case of physical attack, or failure to thrive in a rehabilitation environment due to intimidation.

We know that we have real obstacle in the prison system without doubt
A rehabilitation endeavor has become a country club for bodybuilders
A realm of reluctantly converted homosexuals corrupted or broken for life
Though we crave rehabilitation while serving up only forced debauchery

How well do we protect those we force under our care for their trespasses

Mock and laugh at the world we created for the most vile to the most meek

A sameness that we who send them could not flourish in or so fail miserably

Are we asking for a bumper crop of wheat from mere seeds of weeds adrift

We reject the finish products of what our prisons are returning for our investment

A fortune invested repeatedly for the same previously invested fortune

Do we expect any better when we send the same child back to finishing school

The same finishing school meant to prepare them for society - fails repeatedly

Admit that our investment went and continues to go up in smoke over and over

Change the school that has failed society and those we sent to be overhauled

Change the school and change the student and we may even change society

Prisons are schools needing accreditation in order to maintain a competent teaching staff constantly teach the teachers while teaching the students. Sadistic and non compassionate individuals need not apply for staff positions, skilled or unskilled.

The brown stranger offered an approach to the prison problem of high rate of revisitism in the system. He suggested a mass release of nonviolent inmates imprisoned for use and non trafficking possession of drugs. Saying they should be released immediately on parole and required to volunteer for the governor's rehabilitation program as part of a parole agreement. Funding for such a program would be done with the monies no longer needed for incarcerating them and also some money may be used to address prison conditions not conducive to true rehabilitation.

Nonviolent addiction is a real disease to be reckoned with at some point
Turning nonviolent into violent creatures is creating monsters let loose
Monsters we can expect when nonviolent offenders are placed among corruption
Are we the (Frankenstein) that created the system that made the monster?

Creators must continue to create and improve because failure breeds itself
Left alone failure shall reproduce and grow uncontrolled until it rules the makers
Makers are left to change and recreate or chose to go blind and hard of hearing
We manage our crops, families and in most cases our lives, let us now do society

Managing our fears of society may lead to a more dear society for all living within
Can most walk the streets at night or in a strange neighborhood at anytime
If we respond negatively to either then we do have fears of a society not as dear
Change our ways of administering justice in a world bent on bending it for profit

Some are meant for prison but not all doing life need a lifelong sentence
Rehabilitation may be achieved in more instances than we currently experience

Separate the monster makers from the body parts needed to maintain makers

Give each a path to freedom or a path to incarceration with essential comforts

The brown stranger's recommendations that a stone and steel place of incarceration be shown and explained to all entering its system as a place of contemplation and reformation of anti social activities. No tolerance for mischief, abuse of any sort and non - adherence to rules. Infractions shall include isolation from any who may be harmed physically or psychologically. No shortening of a sentence shall be considered for any who fail in the aforementioned. Those incarcerated for life may find themselves in total isolation from others, in order to assure the safety of all inmates. A slogan must be adopted "Live in peace together or live alone".

Prisons housing only those in need of incarceration for rehabilitation
Shall be the focus of the reeducated and often evaluated prison staff
A physical force team on call all hours as an armed response team
A now safe environment for staff as well as inmates to grow together

Inmates grow together along with staff or live apart from other inmates
Choices are given and respected and each inmate held accountable
A realm in which inmates lives are entirely in the choices they make
Growing and rehabilitating in opposition to defiant and antisocial ways

Giving hope to those without hope who have been seasoned in crime
Showing that a mending of ways may reintroduce one to his society
Or they can spend their days in incarceration or isolation if appropriate
A choice of living free or living in a vat of society's stagnation of sewage

Welcomed to society or banished as applied by the courts or returned so

No rights or amenities just the essentials of humanity given to live enough

Never allow a life on the inside to be preferable to living free in society

Incarceration should be a punishment and reconciliation for society's sores

Donald defined: Gaelic (Brown Stranger)

Acknowledgement to my wife who is also my favorite writer and editor Ruth Elaine Young. Whose encouragement and support made this book possible.

Printed and bound by PG in the USA

USA2018PGIL